Date Due

BRODART, CO.   Cat. No. 23-233   Printed in U.S.A.

EUROPE

LONDON

VENICE

ROME

ISTANBUL

CAPPADOCIA

DAMASCUS

JERASH

KERMANS

BAGHDAD

JERUSALEM.

TE

SHIRA

SAUDI
ARABIA

K

KH

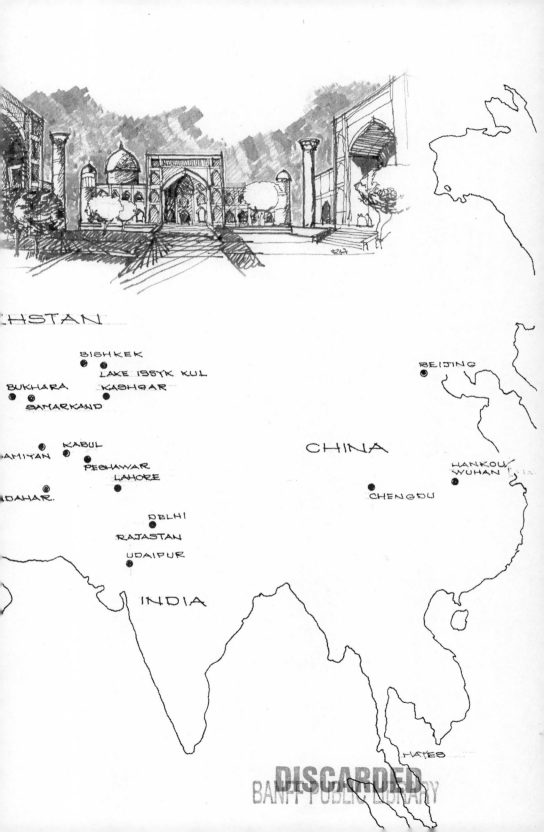

HSTAN

BISHKEK
LAKE ISSYK KUL
BUKHARA   KASHGAR
SAMARKAND

BEIJING

CHINA

KABUL
AMIYAN
PESHAWAR
LAHORE
DAHAR.

HANKOU/
WUHAN
CHENGDU

DELHI
RAJASTAN
UDAIPUR

INDIA

HATES

Weaving Threads

Travels on the Silk Road

NANCY M. HAYES

DRAWINGS BY ROSS E. HAYES

SMALL
BATCH
BOOKS

493 SOUTH PLEASANT STREET
AMHERST, MASSACHUSETTS 01002
413.230.3943
SMALLBATCHBOOKS.COM

For our children,
Sarah, Michael, and Erin,
and our grandchildren,
Ava, Taylor, Charlie, and William

ACKNOWLEDGMENTS

*M*Y DEEPEST GRATITUDE is to the people I have met during the course of my travels, who are the subject of this, my first, book. Their generous hospitality, friendship, and help, when we needed it, are my inspiration.

This book wouldn't have been written without the love and wisdom of my parents, Mary and Bill Phené, and parents-in-law, Eve and Chuck Hayes, who so long ago saw promise, kept our letters, and encouraged the path I chose. My sisters, Carol MacLeod and Jeanne Phené, as well as many good friends, urged me to record my stories, and I am grateful to them for spurring me on. Later, workshops at the Banff Centre helped me unravel my writing.

I made it to the finish line with the support of Easy Writers — Elena Aitken, Trish Loye Elliot, Leanne Shirtliffe, and Bradley Somer — the best, kindest, and most constructive critics on earth. The expert and thoughtful guidance of Fred Levine of Small Batch Books helped *Weaving Threads* finally reach its destination — you, the reader. Thank you.

Most of all I want to thank Ross, whose love and happy spirit made my journey happen.

— N.M.H.

CONTENTS

nomads on the silk road

I

parachuting to the silk road

"A written word is the choicest of relics.
It is something at once more intimate with us
and more universal than any other work of art.
It is the work of art nearest life itself."

FROM *WALDEN*
BY HENRY DAVID THOREAU

*T*HIS IS MY STORY about travel along the Silk Road, as near life as I can make it. I didn't know when I started out that it was a journey that would last a lifetime.

I can still smell the streets of Kabul. I breathe in the tang of dung smouldering under charred cook pots and the stench of fresh, wet mud applied to new buildings as I sit here trying to make sense of the experience. Beside me is a small blue suitcase covered in dust. Inside, maps that mark the route we took are faded and crisp. Rubber bands around stacks of pamphlets and letters I wrote my mother are disintegrating.

I pull out my green travel journal with the pages falling apart and read, "September 1965. Kabul. Lovely but rough drive through the Hindu Kush mountains to Bamiyan. Nomadic encampments in the valleys. People dressed in reds, blacks, with silver sparkling jewellery." And then I pick up a crumbling tourist brochure and read, "Afghanistan is a land of sunshine with an extremely healthy climate. Its famous and historic sites and amazing local colour provide a fascinating and thrilling experience for every traveller."

It was an exaggeration, propaganda perhaps, but the Silk Road between Europe and China was beautiful, and it was thrilling for me to discover it.

People are curious and ask me, "What do you mean? Silk Road?" or "Why do you want to go there?"

Long before television came, children like me played around a big wooden radio, the centre of the living room.

The crackly sound in the background is CBC's *Saturday Afternoon at the Opera*. Music and strange-sounding words from far away are a stage to take me around the world to places in Europe and the Orient where, through play, I learn about life.

My dress-up clothes are silk. Silk parachutes. Dad works in a munitions factory. After the war, he brought home some grubby white parachutes and said, "We won't need them

2

anymore. Mom said you'd like to play with them." (I was thrilled, but it was Mom's passion for those parachutes that surprised me, even today. Remembering.)

"HOT DYE. Watch out!" she screams when I get too close to watch her pile them into the biggest pots we have, full of bubbling, boiling dye. I jump back and reposition myself to look at her carefully squeezing in new life, like magic, transforming them into colourful clothing for my imaginary travels.

In those days, I didn't know it was silk — strong, mysterious, and coveted by rich Roman matrons — that sparked exchange between Europe and the Orient in the first century. Before long, trade began to thrive, and for the next 2,000 years, a network of corridors between the two continents was built up. By the end of the nineteenth century, these intertwining paths became informally known as the "Silk Road."

The routes crossed some of the highest mountain passes and bleakest deserts on earth. Why would I not travel there? After all, I had been travelling the Silk Road for years in my imaginary play.

Marco Polo was seventeen when he set out on his travels, in 1271. Even though he went 700 years before me, I think I understand how he felt. Scared, a bit homesick, but keen to learn. He went with his father and uncle to search for an easy overland route between Italy and China so they could buy precious silk to sell in Europe. Marco ended up staying in China, and twenty-four years later, he returned to

Italy by sea. Some of the corridors he crossed were the same ones travelled by Alexander and Genghis Khan, and years later the account of his explorations motivated Christopher Columbus.

I was twenty-four when I set out for adventure with my husband, Ross. Along those rough gravel roads, I carried on with my education that began with parachutes and opera. The route we took twisted through Europe and snaked across the furnace of connected deserts and oasis towns in the Middle East and Iran. Then it continued east, toward China and India, over the central part of Asia through steppes, fertile valleys, and rugged mountain ranges.

After an unexpected encounter with war in Pakistan, refuge in Afghanistan, and an Iron Curtain blockade in the Soviet Union, Ross and I went back to Canada, promising ourselves that one day we would return. To help fill the gap in our unfinished Silk Road travel, four decades later we continued our adventure in China, India, and the Central Asian "stans" of the former Soviet Union.

"Did anything bad happen? You sound as though it were a fairy tale. It can't be just like that," some people say. Well, they're right. Some of the stories still disturb me when I recall them. I've shed more than a few tears over the years. But what I want to tell you most is about the goodness in people I met along the way.

4

IRKESHTAM
PASS

intrepid mods with their vespa, 1964

II

su*rp*rises (ᴇɴɢʟᴀɴᴅ)

*M*Y HOROSCOPE SAYS, "You will have a surprise today, and you won't know whether to be happy or not." That's so true. Ross surprised me with a new plan for us when he came home from work, and I'm having a hard time figuring out whether to be happy or not.

We both graduated from university one month ago. We got married the following week. The day after the wedding, we boarded the *Franconia*, an enormous ocean liner, and waved a distraught goodbye to our families. We sailed down the St. Lawrence, out through the Gulf, and then crossed the Atlantic. Seven days later, we arrived in London and started new jobs right away.

Ross is an architect at Arup Associates and is studying for a masters degree in urban planning at University College London at night. I work for the London County Council as a school nursing–sister in Camden Town. "Sista Eyes," they call me, dropping the "h," and I love it.

Our home is one large yellow room in Mrs. Gyll's house.

7

We've got a one-burner hot plate for cooking, one small cot for sleeping, and a tiny bathroom under the stairs that we share with a half dozen other people. We're lucky. After twenty years, London is still wresting itself from the devastation of war, and housing is scarce.

For the pleasantly rounded, rosy-cheeked, glamorous Mrs. Gyll, the war is always present. She was a star actress in Hollywood but returned home to London to do what she could to help the war effort. She drove an ambulance during the Blitz.

"It was always night," she declares in strong, carefully enunciated words. "The German rockets were launched from France, and when the sky lit up, we could see it was filled with enemy planes and Spitfires. London was on fire. But it's the escalator I can't forget. People ran to the Tube stations. They were supposed to be safe shelters." Her smile disappears, and in a defeated, quiet voice she tells us, "One really awful night, everyone panicked. When I got there, dozens were dead, lying on top of each other. On the escalator."

I weep inside and say nothing.

(To this day, forty-five years later, Mrs. Gyll's story grips me when I step onto a long escalator and think of the people that night. I wish I could tell her again that I'm in awe of her courage and bravery.)

I think my life is almost perfect.

Then Ross comes home from work and says, "I met a fellow in the office today who hitchhiked here all the way from Pakistan. A fantastic trip."

I freeze. I can feel what's coming next.

"He said the trip was easy. Things there are fairly stable. Next year it may not be. We should go now."

"Now? Right now? Leave London? We just arrived. I'm not even unpacked."

"So it won't be a problem, we won't have to unpack. We can just send our stuff back to Montreal." Ross's easy and confident manner is partly why I married him, but this time he has gone too far.

"Hitchhike? Why?" Desperately, I try to choke back anger toward my true love and his stupid idea.

"Hitchhiking would be fun. We'll meet lots of people. It wouldn't cost anything."

"No. We'd get ourselves killed. Definitely no. I can't go."

"Maybe we could buy a scooter. Secondhand. We still have the wedding present money."

"That money is for china. English bone china. And speaking of dishes, just what are we going to eat? We don't have any money. Where is Pakistan, anyway?" Those opera singers I listened to on the radio never went to Pakistan.

"The fellow that went has maps. We could work here and there along the way."

"How can we work? We don't even know the language. I'd have to get another license. Remember? I'm a nurse. I need a license. And I want to work here. You've lived here before. London," I sneer. "You liked it. I'm staying here. I told the director I would stay two years."

Ross tenses up, his sweet smile changes. "What I'm telling you, right now, is that it's peaceful between India and Pakistan. It may not last. It could be our only chance to travel the Silk Road between Europe and Asia."

"So why can't we cut our time here short and leave next year?"

"Well, we could do it that way. We could buy the scooter now, practise driving around England, and leave next summer."

"So. We'll leave Europe and head east on a scooter? Like Marco Polo without the camels?"

I can't believe it. My horoscope was right. I'm struggling with whether to be happy or not with the surprise change of plans.

We work on merging each of our life agendas so that we both can be happy. Learning the art of negotiation—listening, considering, giving a little, taking back, and then giving more—is not easy. I try to inform myself by reading Ross's textbook *A History of Architecture,* by Banister Fletcher. The British Automobile Association supplies us with maps, complete with "comments on roads, regulations, and interesting details," fresh from covert study of the Middle East and Asia during the war.

Nepal is closed to visitors, but Ross thinks we probably could sneak into the country somehow. "But let's go to Afghanistan first," he says.

"Where's it?"

"On the way to India, northwest of Nepal, in the Hindu Kush mountains. People have been going there for centuries. Alexander took his armies there, so did Timur,

Babur, Genghis Khan. You name it. All the star warriors went. Even the British. The Afghans managed to kick them all out."

"Okay. Let's put Afghanistan on the list."

"Then we could head south and stay for a year in India to work and make money to keep going on. It's impossible to get across the border into China right now anyway, but that may change soon. We'll be flexible."

We buy an old scooter, a Vespa. Ross calls it "Fifi." He would prefer a BMW motorcycle.

We practise riding to India by scootering the streets of London. They're not gravel roads like in Asia; cobble will have to do. I perch myself behind Ross, holding on for dear life as he shouts behind that he's taking me to the bank district to see where the new Disney movie we saw last night was filmed. It's early Saturday morning, sun is beginning to break the cold shadow of office towers, and I feel like I'm part of the movie. A handful of people are walking around with shopping bags, scattering pigeons as they go. One scooter is making its own statement clattering along the cobble. That's us. Is Mary Poppins here too?

Today as I write, I can still feel Ross's warm body against mine and his heart thumping through a thick wool sweater as he scooters me around, gently teaching me to enjoy the unexpected and believe in magic. That year, we explored everywhere within scootering distance of London.

We tested our new camping equipment. I smile whenever I see that old Black's Good Companion tent sitting on our basement shelf. At the time, it was high tech, and we were proud of it. Now its faded and worn cotton, with the oilskin floor and makeshift mosquito net I sewed inside intact, still stirs my pride.

Sometimes we spend weekends with friends who have real cars, and we travel farther — to the Lake District for hiking, to Liverpool to look at innovative housing projects and see if we can steal a glimpse of the Beatles, the new rock band. We're learning to be envious. Car travel is luxurious and easy.

We drive the scooter along the M's, the M5 and the M100, in noisy slow motion. Jeeps, lorries, and motorcycles fly past us, but scooters do not. We can stand the bumps, the cold, and the noise for only an hour at a time, and our voices are hoarse and sore with shouting back and forth, so we decide we should try a scooter stamina test abroad. We'll go to what the English call "the Continent." We'll go to the Lausanne World Art Exhibit. "It's not far," says Ross, "just across the Channel."

The fields are sunny, the wine is cheap, the picnics are long and romantic, but the highway is endless. A sign indicates that Lausanne is east, and Paris, closer, is west. The choice is obvious. We choose Paris.

And buy a car when we get back to London.

We've worked long hours and saved our money. Adding this to our wedding-gift account, we now have $1,450 to buy a new, tax-free Beetle. We will be the modern Marco Polo couple. We'll do the Silk Road by car and buy tickets to return to Europe by sea the following year.

We arrange for new jobs in Delhi.

And I have a new respect for horoscopes. *Surprise* (verb): (1) to catch someone unaware; (2) to cause somebody to feel wonder or amazement; (3) to make an unexpected gift to someone.

I love it all.

Ross's surprise that year has lasted almost half a century.

my parents and me, rome

I I I

saying goodbye (europe)

ROME, 1965. The grand Global Bus Tour is ready to leave, and through a cloud of fumes I choke back tears. Then I look up. There's Dad looking out the window crying, trying not to. He turns his head away from me, toward Mom, who's sitting on the bus next to him. Mom is muffling a nervous-looking sort of laugh. She points and beckons me to look at the other passengers, their new friends, staring out the window at us, some grim faced, some keeping Dad company crying.

I see Mom struggling to keep herself together. She ought to; she's the one who's been encouraging all this travel. "You need to remember the parachutes," she had said not long ago. "You've been rehearsing this for a long time now. Don't worry. You'll be okay."

Ross, standing with his arm around me, looks bewildered, not knowing what to do, wanting to make everything right. It strikes me that it is odd Mom and Dad are the ones who are going away, but I am the one who is leaving.

Pangs of separation hurt.

Earlier that spring, our families and friends had come from Quebec, a few at a time, to visit us in London and say goodbye before we left for the Silk Road. And oblivion, I thought. The last guests to arrive were my parents, who were leaving from London to go on a bus tour of Europe. We agreed to meet them again in Venice after dropping off some things we wouldn't need with my cousins in Normandy. Then we would follow Mom and Dad and their bus around Italy before saying goodbye to them in Rome.

Leaving London is a blur now. As it was then. A blur of frantic preparation and fragmented farewells. I made lists. I still do. Lots of lists. I had lists to solve every kind of emergency — car breakdown, medical crises, and starvation. I made a list of Canadian embassies and consulates we could contact in every country and another list of official papers we needed to obtain from foreign embassies in London that would get us through borders. Our most precious and difficult-to-obtain document was the triptyque, a thick, multipage pile of certificates that gave us permission to temporarily take the Beetle into each country.

Except Iraq.

"It's a dictatorship. That means there are no rules. So no triptyque," Ross says. His look tells me he doesn't know whether to be happy about his release from having to deal with another difficult embassy or devastated that the Iraq border might be as far as we get.

"What are our options?"

"We'll paint a red cross on top of the car and see where it gets us."

"It won't get us anywhere. We need a red crescent."

We laugh. Being naive has advantages. What we don't know can't worry us.

We go to appointments with doctors and dentists to eliminate all potential catastrophes. Wisdom teeth are removed and serums are injected.

We mail the new English bone china home.

We attend farewell parties.

On July 1, 1965, we take a long drive to northern Scotland to bid a final goodbye to Aunt Daisy, my grandmother's youngest and favourite sister. Aunt Daisy's frail, curled-up body belies her youthful spirit. From her bed in the nursing home she's been confined to for years, her laughter and happy stories inspire me. And dare me to seek adventure.

When we get back to London, we cram all our belongings into the Beetle and inch our way out of the city.

("How did you feel about leaving London?" friends ask me now. To be honest, what I remember feeling the most is a giant paper Japanese lantern I held on my lap. I didn't want to leave it behind.)

Roses and a small apple orchard surround Guy and Simone's faux Tudor house in Normandy. Guy is a distant cousin of my father's, and when he was a young man, he lived for a year with Dad and his family in Toronto. He and Simone are keen to repay the kindness and have taken good care of us this year.

"Ahh. Nancy *et* Ross. *Entrez, entrez.* Come in. So glad you're here again. *Mais non*, this time you are saying goodbye."

I take a deep breath of sweet-smelling Normandy air. It is good to be here, to be pampered in the warmth of family.

A few metres from the orchard are a vegetable garden and a murky green pond. Guy told us on our first visit that the pond was used for raising fish during the war. There wasn't much food. "Our family was lucky," Guy had said. "We grew our own."

Most of the time, their house was crowded with boarders. Some of them soldiers. Here, a few kilometres from the Normandy coast and the port city of Le Havre, they were safer from the bombs and they survived. Memories of the horrors of war are painful to talk about, and I've learned this year that my probes and questions are best left until the time is right. One day when we are driving with Guy through a tunnel near Le Havre, he says casually that during the war, when the British bombed the tunnel, Uncle Herbert was killed. I am stunned into silence. There are some things I don't want to know more about, and that is one of them. It hurts too much.

Today we are not here to talk about war; we are here for a family party. Guy ducks his head, scurries down into the cellar, and quickly comes back up the stairs, cradling something in his arms. "Ahh. Look what I've found. A good bottle of champagne, to wish you bon voyage."

We move into the living room, toast our family, and begin sharing stories. Chantal, the youngest of the family, is bubbling over with excitement; her boyfriend is coming over later this evening. "It looks serious," says Simone with a shrug. Elizabeth, the middle sister, has done well in her final ophthalmology exams recently and is excited about her new job with a local optometrist. Marie Jose, the eldest sister, has an intensely serious air about her. She should. She arrived from Le Mans a few minutes ago in her flameproof suit—her passion is car racing.

I struggle to keep up with overlapping exclamations about family characters, fast vehicles, and food. Eventually, I migrate with the girls toward the smell of roast beef cooking. In the kitchen, the biggest, sunniest room in the house, we all work together under Simone's quiet tutelage. Our female assembly line prepares dinner while comfortably seated around a big wooden table laden with freshly picked berries, tiny vegetables from the garden, and long thin loaves of crusty bread. The sound of pots clanking and girls chattering lulls me into a state of nostalgia. Traditional Sunday dinners with family are what I miss the most, and I am in heaven here in my French home.

Hours later, I wrestle with the night and try to calm my anxiety. So if this is heaven, why am I leaving?

After early morning hugs, a kiss on each cheek, and then another kiss for good measure, we climb into the Beetle, this time with only what we would need for the Silk Road. (I have the lists of things we took in front of me as I write today.) Food—Vesta dried dinners, bottles of concentrated orange juice, several pounds of good, dark-roast coffee, and vitamins. Pills—antidiarrhoeal, antimalarial, and antibiotic. Camping—tent, sleeping bags, pots, table, stools, table-cloth and napkins, and a new Italian espresso coffeepot. Finances—we cleaned out our bank accounts: $839. It was to last us four months, until we got our first paycheques in India.

Like a cathedral, columns of Lombardy poplars received our little procession as we waved goodbye, worked our way across the country, and drove out of France.

Marco Polo came of age in Venice, a city-state of 118 small islands connected by bridges and tiny waterways. In the thirteenth century it was the place where the West met the East and was filled with merchants coming and going in their search for silk and jewels to trade. It was dark, wet, and filled with superstition, sin, and sinking buildings. (I suppose it was an expensive city to live in then too.)

It didn't occur to me that we couldn't simply drive into Venice and camp somewhere near the centre. Ross explained that Venice's geography hadn't changed since Marco's time, that it has never had cars, and that we would have to camp several kilometres outside the city.

My vision of romantic Venice is shattered. Our campsite is cheap, dirty, and overcrowded. Last night it rained; our supposedly high-tech waterproof tent flooded. Everything is wet. Haughty campers, the ones with the big trailers, sneer and stare at us mopping up our soggy disaster. I want to scream at them, I'm here to say goodbye. To my parents. Like Marco Polo did in 1271.

Did he feel like I do? Did he ask himself why he was leaving?

My fairy-tale visions have disappeared, and all I see is oblivion, emptiness on the road ahead.

Vaporetti, the motorboats, and gondolas are the modus operandi for the rich in Venice. I walk, trying to restore the fairy tales. Rain has tempered the tourist invasion; I lose myself in the romance of the city. As we pick our way through pigeons and wet, dark alleys, the stories of Venice's history and architecture come alive for Ross and me.

Late in the afternoon, the sky begins to clear, and I start to panic that we won't be able to find Mom and Dad. I've lost my list. The name of their hotel is on it.

"Don't worry so much, Nance. We'll just walk around until we find them. They'll be looking for us too. In fact, the whole bus will be looking for us. Look over there. Gondoliers don't work when it's raining, and there's another gondola. That must mean the rain has stopped for today."

We round another corner and see a bunch of soggy, confused-looking tourists crawl out of a gondola and cram into our alley. We stop to let them squeeze by. I'm taken aback. That tall, confident-looking guy with the high forehead and small mustache looks familiar. His gnarled face is white, like a ghost, and his pale blue eyes stare at me in disbelief. It's Dad. He and Mom have just arrived.

21

The pattern for the next few days is a flurry of travel through northern and central Italy to Rome with Mom and Dad in their bus, Ross and I close behind in the Beetle.

Vineyards, green hills, and olive groves flash by. Ancient hill towns beg us to stay longer. We speak our version of Italian and croon love songs we know from the opera to each other.

We entertain.

Sunroofs like ours on the Beetle are new contraptions. They set the stage for us to pop out into the sun to holler and wave to children and farmworkers along the road and to all our new friends watching us out the bus window.

In the evenings, the four of us gather in the busiest local café we can find on whatever main plaza to soak up Italian life and warm summer breezes. Dad is our art expert, and Ross tells us about the architecture. Mom and I stick to talking about people and food.

On that trip Ross developed a fine taste for Campari and soda that lasted a lifetime. I'm looking at the photographs from that time, which prove the fun we had. We are standing in front of the Vatican laughing, arm in arm. I am in the middle, with Mom and Dad on each side. We are dressed for the occasion. Dad has on a crisp white dress shirt and dark trousers. He's holding the movie camera. Where are those movies now? Mom's hair is carefully coiffed, and she has on a perky green sundress, a shawl, and a long, fake pearl necklace. Her collapsible hat, I remember, is in the big purse she has around her arm. I have short, curly hair, a brown sundress, a scarf, and a long, brown plastic necklace. I have a hat too—it's in that big leather bag around my shoulder.

Every once in a while I am taken aback when I see so clearly that I am my mother's daughter. I have a hard time believing that Mom was only forty-five years old then. About the same age as my babies are now.

The engine roars, and in big black puffs of diesel exhaust the bus leaves the narrow street—with my parents. I'm devastated.

I turn and walk with Ross a few metres to the plaza at the corner, the Spanish Steps. A fatherly-looking *poliza locale* taps Ross on the shoulder and asks gently, "Excuse, *por favore*. What is the matter? Why is the lady crying? Have you lost something? Can I help?"

I sob, try to recover my composure and be civil. "No. No. Thank you. I'm okay. It's my parents. I've just said goodbye. I won't see them for a long time."

"My wife just needs something to eat," Ross says. I'm pleased he's beginning to understand my quirks. "As soon as she eats, she'll feel better. Can you recommend a good restaurant close by? Not too expensive?"

"Yes, yes, I understand. My wife is the same. You see over there?" He points to a red, green, and white awning in the middle of a narrow street off the plaza. I can almost smell the tomatoes and garlic sautéing from where I stand. "That's where I go," says the policeman. "The family who run it are very nice and the food is delicious. You'll feel better soon."

(I will never forget that simple meal—a glass of good red wine, fresh green salad, and thinly sliced, boiled veal tongue served with a fine brown sauce and capers.)

We sit at a small table with a red chequered tablecloth and candles. The servers are cheerful and keenly interested in why we're visiting. They understand family.

For the moment, the pleasure of being with them eases the pain of saying goodbye.

sultan ahmed mosque, istanbul

IV

fitting (TURKEY)

Fitting: to be in harmony with; adapt.
THE CONCISE OXFORD DICTIONARY, 1995

*I*T IS DIFFICULT FOR ME to bring my memories to the present and choose the right words to explain what it was like for me, at first, to try to fit in with other people along the Silk Road. The beautiful Christmas music I'm listening to this morning helps because it connects me back to the place where early Christians lived and the place in Turkey I want to write about, Cappadocia. There, beginning in the fourth century, early Christians, to escape their persecutors, hid in caves, where they lived in relative harmony for centuries.

Finally we are nearing the crossroads into Asia after days of travel through Italy and Greece. We set up our tent at the BP MoCamp behind the gas station outside Istanbul. I know I am supposed to be starry-eyed and in love like the song the Four Lads have been singing on the radio every day since 1953 — "Istanbul was Constantinople . . . Now it's Turkish delight on a moonlit night" — but for as far as I can see there is black diesel smoke with old cars and gaudy painted trucks jamming the road. Gridlock cuts romance.

I need to refocus. Forget the romance.

Melting in the heat and stink, I force myself to buck up and stick to the mission here: We need to collect our mail that was to be sent to the American Express office in downtown Istanbul.

Finally we get there, and I'm happy that the office takes me back to civilization; it's in the newly built Hilton Hotel, set in acres of trees and gardens. We pick up a paltry pile of two letters. Our mothers have written. I ache for more news, but phoning is out of the question, English newspapers are rare, and telegrams are inadequate. I'm homesick and need a cure. We make another budget adjustment; a fancy drink at the hotel bar should fix me.

The quiet contemporary design smoothes the chaos outside and soothes me. There it is, just across the strait outside the bar's dark sunglass-type windows: Asia. The Bosphorus is vibrant, glistening with ships of every sort gliding silently between Europe and Asia, some toward the east and the Black Sea, others toward the west, the Aegean and the Mediterranean.

I can understand why young Marco had a grand vision of Constantinople. The Venetians had been very successful plundering its riches, and exotic marble columns and pedestals adorned the Piazza San Marco in Venice where he played when he was growing up. Nonetheless, when he first arrived in Constantinople, he was shocked and disappointed. Following conventional wisdom of Europeans of the time, he regarded people who were incomprehensible and different from himself with disdain. He said the people in Constantinople lived like beasts, were ignorant, and "had a barbarous language." In time, he overcame his distaste and enjoyed being there while he waited for the right time to leave.

Marco waited months. Like today, in those times Europe and Asia were not always friendly toward each other, and Constantinople was akin to a swinging door between the two continents, with people running out and back. Marco finally went through the door and left when there was a period of relative peace and hope for safe passage.

We've done the Grande Bazaar and Topkapi Seraglio Palace. We've spent hours in the Blue Mosque, reading and sketching. Now that I've refuelled my courage, I want to step through Istanbul's swinging door like Marco Polo did and leave.

Europe breaks away and Asia begins when we cross the Bosphorus. It is an abrupt shift. Villages made entirely of earth and straw dried in the sun dot vast yellow and brown fields. From tall blue-tiled minarets scattered all around the countryside, muezzins, the mosque officials, wail five times every day calling the faithful to prayer. Men walk along the roadside to the mosque or fields (where they will pray outdoors, facing Mecca, if there is no mosque at hand), and women dressed in dark robes lag behind, carrying their babies.

Marco had to learn to fit in with others' cultures. And so do I. My shorts and sleeveless tank top are abandoned for a faded, long-sleeve orange shirt and a modest green skort, a funny-looking knee-length skirt that covers shorts. This is my travel uniform, and I wear it every day. I memorize ten Turkish words so I can, with a little charade, talk with other women and children in hellos, thank-yous, and goodbyes. And like the Turkish women, I walk behind my man.

Eventually, the brown and yellow fields shift to lush green mountains. The road twists through the Bolu Pass and then out onto a fertile plateau. In time, the road changes direction again, and we continue over a parched mountain range to a barren land of dry valleys, sandstone cliffs, and salt flats.

This is Cappadocia, where early Christians carved villages into the cliffs. It was a good hiding place for them. So good, we can't find it.

The moonlike landscape, nameless roads, and map tell us nothing of where to find the ancient dwellings Ross has read about in his architectural texts. In fact, now we are lost. We reach a small village, Nevshir, and ask where we can camp for the night. A young man our age speaks a little French, gets the drift of our question, and smiling happily, along with a group of about twenty young men who have suddenly joined us, leads us to the local high school.

"There," they beam with pride. "That's where our guests sleep." It is a clean, almost empty classroom, and in the corner is a double bed frame with a spring. No mattress. Lots of chalk dust.

My heart sinks and my brain goes into action trying to figure how this will work.

(Could I have known then that this would be an oddly reoccurring scene as we tried to find safe places to sleep across Asia?)

Our pickup hosts are enthusiastic and exude hospitality, and we need help finding the caves, so I quash down my fear and resist complicating the situation by refusing to sleep in the classroom. With curious eyes watching, we unload our air mattress and sleeping bag onto the spring before we all march down the road to the village restaurant for supper.

The food is "worth a journey," to steal a few words from a popular guidebook that says nothing about this restaurant. Turkey, with its diverse agriculture and society, is a gastronome's paradise. I don't know who is doing the cooking; I have yet to see another woman in this town, but whoever prepared the charcoal-grilled lamb kebabs, steamed rice pilaf, savoury lentils, hot pita bread, salad, and yoghurt is a master chef.

After dinner, we accept an invitation to go to one of our new friends' home for tea and music. A kind of Turkish lute, the *saz*, and a percussion instrument accompany our companions' voices singing soulful lyrics. The lads are shy and look right past me, the only woman present, and I am left to wonder alone what the words they are singing might mean. All conversation and questions are directed to Ross. To be honest, I'm grateful I'm here, safely sinking into nonexistence. Ignored. This is my time to watch and think. I fit in just by being silent.

Marco Polo travelled for twenty-four years on the tangled routes between Europe and China. When he returned to Italy, people were amazed with his stories, and eventually his friend Rusticello wrote them down. The book, *Il Millione*, enthralled Europeans for centuries. Telling stories over and over, remembering the lessons we learn, each with our own perspective, is a vital part of living.

One winter evening not long ago, as our family sat by the fire listening to each other tell stories about Turkey, Ross said, "When I think back to our first time in Turkey, in 1965, it really strikes me as an amazing time. Remember? We woke up to this unbelievable sound coming from the minaret, and there I was in a schoolroom under a blackboard. We were covered in chalk dust. Then I remembered where I was and the concert the night before. We didn't know what was going on; we were totally tired, but it was a special performance for us. Not that we were special, but we were interested in them. We were the only two guests. The mayor was there. It was the weirdest damn thing. But we wanted to hear them. We took it as it came.

"Then there was the time in 1990 when we went with you kids," he continued. "We were exploring, and this lady came up to us with all that fruit. To this day, I can picture it. We were apprehensive, but she came up to us from nowhere and said, 'Welcome to my country.' We don't welcome people coming from Scotland or wherever to Lake Louise, do we?"

When we returned to Turkey in 1990 with our three adult children, our lives were in transition. After years of family adventure (which is the subject of another story), the kids were leaving home, and we were worried there wouldn't be another chance for the five of us to vacation together. Sarah, after living in Europe and Eastern Canada for the past six years, had completed an honours degree in political science and was excited about returning home to Calgary and starting her first full-time job. Michael, a competitive cyclist, was in third-year engineering in Edmonton. Erin, recently returned from a nine-month sailing trip around the Pacific, would be starting a degree in physical education in the fall. With their multitalents, Ross and I thought they would adapt well to travel life in Turkey. Our plan was to drive to Cappadocia from Istanbul, then charter a boat and sail north up the coast before returning to Istanbul. Admittedly, we had a selfish reason for bringing them along. We needed the crew.

We drove around the country in a battered, no-name rented station wagon that won kudos from the kids by being hand-painted black and unpredictably shooting out steam as it exploded to a stop. They called it the hearse.

"What I remember about that trip," Sarah recalled, "was the heat, and going through this whole journey just to get there. There was this feeling of family, all packed into the hearse, each of us fighting discomfort in our own way. We explored together."

The quaint dirt road between Istanbul and Ankara we travelled in 1965 had become a six-lane serpentine, jammed with fast-moving trucks disgorging black, foul-smelling fumes. The little brown villages we had seen on our trip twenty-five years before had morphed into miles of tacky high-rise apartments between minarets. Snowcapped mountains eventually replaced the shoddy high-rises, but the highway continued to snake southward and up through the Bolu Pass. We were cramped, jet-lagged, and cranky as Ross and I tried to convince the kids that the Turkey of our stories was still there, somewhere.

Then, like an apparition from the cosmos, a sign rose from a rocky cliff high above the highway. The kids screamed, "Turn, turn!"

"Overnight Camping," said the faded old sign above the road. We made a quick exit off the highway to a rough gravel track that went under an overpass and along a dirt road to the campsite.

A stout, kindly-looking woman with an apron around her middle and a kerchief on her head welcomed us as the sun began to set behind the 3,000-metre-high mountain range. She said, approximately, in Turkish that she was pleased to be of service. We were the first Canadian family to stay. We pitched our tents and laid out thin cotton sheets that, in my wisdom, I insisted we pack instead of bulky down sleeping bags. After all, who would need sleeping bags in Turkey in August?

The sun set and summer vanished.

"It was so cold that night," Erin said. "When we thought you and Dad were asleep, we put our headlamps on and ran up the mountain in the moonlight to keep warm." Creative adaptation came naturally to the kids.

None of us slept that night. But we laughed a lot.

We checked out at 5:00 a.m.; we were stopped by the highway patrol at 5:05 a.m. Ross paid his dues to the unpleasant cop and then, undeterred by extortion, sped off again to the first roadside truck stand along the way for breakfast.

"No recipe for that scrumptious hot lentil soup could restore the experience," Sarah said. "It was wonderful and warm, even though we were shivering in the cold sunshine and surrounded by truck drivers."

"I've selective memory on that one," Michael interjected. "I vividly remember the caves, but I'm trying to forget the runs I had for a month after that breakfast."

When we got to Nevshir, the little provincial town we had visited in 1965, we found it transformed into a grand destination resort town. European jumbo jets crowded the town's airport runway; giant tour buses ran their engines for air-conditioning in shiny black parking lots; and long lines crammed entrances to main cave sites.

I was awestruck, but not defeated, by progress. Living where we do, we understand how special-destination places like Banff work. A few kilometres off the well-loved paths tourists take are uncluttered natural places. In unison, we launched a new itinerary. We would simply drive out of Nevshir, park the hearse, and hike into the surrounding valley to search for smaller, less-known cave villages.

As we discussed our stories about Turkey, Michael said he remembered the little road where we eventually stopped. "We were totally lost, looking for directions, and then we got out of the car," he said. "I remember thinking that this was the exact same spot that was in your picture with the Beetle and you in that old green skirt and orange shirt you wore all the time. We just stumbled upon that place again. But still I felt like I was discovering it for the first time."

"What I remember most," Erin added, "was how old everything was, and that real people like us had carved those caves and painted those awesome pictures on the wall."

"Those caves were not well known; there were no tourists. I remember Erin and I climbed way up inside this cave bumping our heads on the way," Michael continued. "We're taller than they were in the fourth century. Suddenly, Ali pops his head in. He was a fun kid who wanted to show us his neighbourhood. In fact, it was more than just Ali; he was part of a family too, and he thought it was special that another family would want to visit his country, his place."

"I remember at first we were scared of that kid," Sarah said, "but not Dad or Mike. They trusted him implicitly. Then Ali takes us home to meet his family. That was very special.

People here wouldn't do that. We had to communicate with smiles and gestures."

"Remember," Michael said, "we all sat on the floor around a table while Ali barked orders at his little sister to bring us food. She went about serving us very casually with a big smile on her face. That highlighted the cultural differences for me. My sisters wouldn't serve me."

Erin remembered Ali's sister too. "It was hilarious. Everyone had fun. They took us in to show us their hospitality. They were so happy a family from Canada had come to their home."

"Everyone had ginormous smiles. I haven't thought about that for a long time. It was one of those special places I want to take Ava someday," Sarah said.

In August 1999 the earth opened up and swallowed the six-lane serpentine that wound its way through the Bolu Pass. Seventeen thousand bodies were recovered and 44,000 people were injured. Another quake hit three months later. By that time, although most people left living in the 30,000-square-kilometre area were already living in tent cities, 845 people were killed and 5,000 injured. Of the remaining buildings, 124,000 were destroyed. An average of twelve aftershocks a day hit the area between August and December that year.

It is April 2000. Where are the minarets? Where are the shoddy apartment buildings? As in scenes from a horror movie, devastation lies before me in miles of concrete and asphalt wreckage along the road from Istanbul to Ankara where my meeting is to take place. The aftershocks have lessened now, it is a beautiful spring evening, and I'm here to represent UNICEF Canada and give support. The local fire chief and his men have invited me to a meeting. I'm sitting on a broken white plastic chair under a tree surrounded by rubble. They start by telling me it's an honour to have me visit from Canada and they're grateful for all the help we've given, but it is clear to me that what they really want to do is tell me their stories. To help unburden the horror. Their world has been turned upside down. Loved ones are gone; voices are crying for help; their homes are tombs.

The chief says he was having a shave in the barbershop down the street when the Big One began in December 1999. In a flash, windows began to vibrate wildly as a terrifying rumble gathered intensity; the windows shattered; the power went off. He tore down the main street to his station. As he ran, burning five-story buildings crumbled down around him. Voices were screaming for help. When he got to his station, two of his men were already dead. The rest had started the fire trucks and they sped up to the reservoir to fill the water tanks. They knew the main line would break.

Now, several months later, they're exhausted from working long hours. The firemen tell me no one can sleep anymore. Children can no longer close their eyes. Images of fire and disaster haunt. Eyes are distant, detached.

Blue tent cities lie in acres of gravel and mud puddles. Here, potable water, food, and a sanitation system are available. Although many of the former teachers have fled to Istanbul because they are afraid to live here anymore, new, young teachers who need jobs have arrived to replace them, and there are several tent schools open. Teams of post-trauma syndrome experts have arrived from Norway to work with parents and teachers. I remember Mrs. Gyll telling me how important it was, during the Blitz in London, to get the kids back to school right away, to help them readapt to normal life.

I head down wooden plank walkways between the puddles to a large tent with children's drawings pinned to the canvas outside. From the small voices I hear inside I know this must be the school that is expecting me. I quietly enter and stand in the corner to watch. About twenty six-year-olds are in a circle, lying on their stomachs with their heads tucked down and their hands stretched out in front of them. They are pounding the ground in time to music.

"What were they doing?" I ask the teacher later.

"We have been telling our stories, and now the children are learning to reconnect with the earth again, the earth that misled and hurt them," she says. "To feel the ground and be in harmony with the earth is very important. To learn to feel safe. So that we can fit into a normal life again."

our children with a turkish family

another turkish family in a tent camp following the earthquake

crossing the desert, 1965

V

desert coffee (SYRIA)

*T*HE BATTERED, old aluminum coffee pot filled with warped wooden gadgets that you see on my kitchen counter is special.

One night, we almost used it as a weapon.

"Why are you going there? It's very dangerous," they say. "Whatever you do, don't travel at night. Bedouin will rob you. After they riddle you with bullets."

And so we set off anyway.

The Beetle bumps across a furnace of connected deserts and oasis towns. Everything around us is flat. Hard brown sand glistens like diamonds under a fireball sun.

The heat is unbearable.

I read that Gertrude Bell wore heavy wool to keep out the sun when she crossed this desert on a camel during the First World War. So did Lawrence. We wear bath towels.

Heavy, brown, wet ones. Wet towels over our heads, wet towels over our shoulders, and wet towels across our laps. And then we jam wet brown towels into closed car windows to keep out the hot blast of desert air and block the burning sun.

The sun. The heat. The emptiness. There is so much of nothing here.

It is cooler now; the evening is beautiful and still. A massive orange sun seems unreal to us as it slowly sinks into the sand.

"We really shouldn't camp here," I snap. "They warned it was dangerous. They said don't camp in the desert under any circumstances. Bedouin are everywhere. They're thieves. They'll kidnap us."

"There is no one anywhere near here," Ross says softly. "Why would anyone be here? There's nothing."

He's right. We haven't seen anyone all day. I take a deep breath, calm myself. "Actually, I have to admit I've always wanted to sleep on the desert, under the stars," I whisper.

So here we are. This is the Great Syrian Desert, and like Lawrence of Arabia and Gertrude Bell, we are on our way to explore Palmyra.

Sand the colour of nicely ripe peaches is all around as far as we can see. The heat of the day dissipates as the sun lowers. Dusk begins to settle in. The moon brightens; stars begin to break through day into night, first one, then two, and now a few more. It reminds me of the Christmas story.

We unfold the little Danish wooden camping table,

smooth on the red and white plastic tablecloth, set out our shiny stainless steel cutlery and our brown stoneware coffee cups from Finland. The new Italian coffee pot is popping, sputtering, and exploding, gathering pressure on the little diesel-fuelled camp stove set in the sand. Soon we will have a nice cup of coffee. We have not forgotten to bring all the trappings of what we think is civilization.

"Do you see that?" Ross says, pointing to the darkening night in the east.

"What is it?"

"I don't know. An animal? It looks like a camel."

Black and ghostly, the apparition gathers momentum in a storm of swirling sand. "It's coming toward us. It's someone on a horse," Ross stammers in disbelief.

"It's Bedouin," I screech.

Long, flowing black robes fly in the wind behind him. He holds a wooden staff in his right fist. He raises his arm high. Like a scene from *Lawrence of Arabia*, he is fierce and relentless in his gallop toward us.

"What are we going to do?"

Ross grabs the hot coffee pot. "This'll work."

"What? You'll throw it? At him?"

Months ago we discussed carrying a weapon. Most people we spoke to who crossed this desert carried a gun for protection. We thought about it and decided that if anything bad happened, we would be too scared and inept to shoot anyone. They would shoot us. With our gun.

Now here we are. Scared. Inept. But keen to live. The coffee pot will have to do.

In an explosion of sand, the man reins his horse to a high-speed stop beside us. The coffee pot is poised, ready for action.

But wait a minute. The Bedouin's turban frames a kind, smiling face.

"*Salaam aleikum.*" Peace to you, he says softly.

"Well, now. *Salaam aleikum. Salaam aleikum.* Yes, yes," Ross blurts out, raising the coffee pot in his trembling hands high in the air. "Hey, would you like some coffee?"

The Bedouin smiles broadly again and says something we don't really understand, shoots his arm high in the air, waves, and charges off into the empty, bleak desert.

We are stunned. After a moment, we collapse in laughter. At ourselves.

"He's going somewhere fast. Probably home for supper," Ross says.

Relief and happiness overtake our fear as we lie down in the sand under the stars.

The morning is cold, but the sun is beginning to soar and we know we will be in the furnace again soon. We pack up our little home in the desert and get in the car to leave.

But look.

There he is again. Children are with him, three boys, about ten or twelve, laughing and jostling one another, each on his own magnificent horse. They grind to another of those high-speed horse stops in a cloud of sand, and the man, smiling broadly, gestures that these are his children.

Apparently, they have something special for us.

With Dad's coaching, they shyly deliver us a present. Three freshly picked watermelons.

Their gift has warmed my heart for a lifetime. And I will never throw out that coffee pot.

This morning, I drove from Canmore to the Banff Centre down the Trans-Canada Highway. The road was lined with bright yellow aspens. The sun cast a hue of golden magic on Cascade Mountain.

I was thinking about telling you my story of the Silk Road, the little boys, the watermelons, and our coffee pot. Neil Young was singing on the car radio. Was it by chance for me?

I crossed the ocean for a heart of gold.
I want to be a miner for a heart of gold
It's these expressions I never give
That keep me searching for a heart of gold.
Keeps me searching.*

Salaam aleikum.

---

*Neil Young, "Heart of Gold," *Harvest* (Reprise Records, 1972). Lyrics slightly altered.

palmyra

Jerash, Jordan, 1965

VI

away to the manger
(THE MIDDLE EAST)

*CeW*E'RE ON OUR WAY to Jerusalem, and I think of myself as an expert traveller now. I've slept on the sand in the middle of nowhere and survived. Last week, when we got to Palmyra, an oasis in the middle of the desert since the second century, I walked among Greek colonnades with only the spirits of past residents and explorers beside me. As soon as we emerged from that desert we headed to lush Beirut, where we strolled through markets thriving with all the accoutrements needed for good French cuisine. Smart European shops and sophisticated hotels lined the beach, and we spent hours surfing. It was like heaven for me.

When we got to Damascus I bought a chador to wear so I could enter the great Umayyad Mosque and other Muslim holy places. The long black robe helped me feel safe, part of the community. Later, I walked into another neighbourhood and down the Street Called Straight. Straight from the Bible — King James Version.

Surprises and contradictions are becoming common-place, and I'm feeling fairly smug that I better understand my world, which transforms as I shift between desert and beach, Muslims and Christians, poor and rich.

Late this afternoon, we made it across the border from Syria into Jordan in record time. Now I am in Jerash, serious Bible territory. For Ross, it is serious architectural territory, dating back to the time of Alexander the Great, 332 BC. A giant orange sun floods its rosy glow over Hadrian's triumphal entry arch as we walk around it and rest on top of a little hill so we can take in the peace of the moment. I want to keep this image forever.

"You see? Behind the arch is the Temple of Zeus and beyond that is the hippodrome," Ross points out.

"What's a hippodrome?"

"It's the old sports complex. See the bleachers surround-ing the court? Two-thousand-year-old stone benches — they knew how to build in those days. People are still sitting on them today."

"The other big structure over there looks like a photo from my Latin textbook. It must be the forum. I can almost see the gladiators."

In the distance, walking among the ruins, is a procession of about thirty refined-looking people dressed in multicol-oured traditional Arabic robes.

From our perch, we spot a tidy modern building down the hill, so we get up and walk down a path to it. A man in an official-looking uniform stands by a sign that indicates this is the information pavilion and café. "We are closed for another hour. The president of Sudan is visiting. When he leaves after the reception, we will be able to serve you," he says in broken French.

I am reminded that these Middle Eastern lands have been linked for thousands of years and that Sudan is also one of the earth's oldest civilizations.

Eventually, the president and his entourage leave, and the Jerash official, in a mixture of French and Arabic, invites us to join him in the café, where a small group of men dressed in workers' clothing has gathered.

"Thanks, but first we need to organize a place to stay tonight. I think your brochure says that there are rooms available here," Ross says.

"Yes, of course. You are welcome."

"Can you show us the room? We'd like to wash up, and then we'll join you."

"Yes, of course, but later. The room isn't ready yet," we think he says.

Reluctantly and timidly, we take chairs at a table with the group of bearded, noisy workmen who, by this time, are well into their evening potion of arrack, the strong, liquorice-based Arab liqueur. Ross takes the arrack. I take tea.

Liquorice is not my forte. Neither is Arabic. I wish there were other women here. I miss talking with my girlfriends. I want to talk about family, children, and food. And babies. In fact, I want to talk about anything. I am not an Arab woman, so I am neutered among these men. Of course, if I were an Arab woman, I would be deleted. I wouldn't be here at all. I would be at home. The monotonous murmur of men talking and drinking lulls me to sleep.

I wake up. "What's happening?" Big chairs are being shuffled around. "Where's our room?"

"Here. I think they're saying this is where we sleep. Right here in the café. We all sleep here together."

Ross's voice is shaky. Is he more scared of my reaction or spending the night here, or both?

What can I do? Squash my fear. Ignore the drunken nastiness. Crawl into my own shell. Ross shuffles eight chairs to the corner near the door and lays the sleeping bags on top. I check the door and unlock it. My security is a fast escape.

It's not long before our new friends are all snoring — noisy, wet, grunting snores. Then Ross joins the concert. I keep guard.

The night is long, dark, and cold. Eventually, morning begins to break through the night and Ross opens his eyes.

I struggle to keep my voice to a whisper. "Get. Me. Out. Of. Here."

"Okay. You're right. We've got to leave now while we can."

We gather up the sleeping bags and creep silently out into the early morning light.

(Years later, Ross said to me, "Remember Jerash? We had always thought we would be okay. But I didn't think so that time. Earlier that day, I heard someone talking about how they had given a tourist a hard time. That really freaked me out, even though I guessed that the traveller was just being an arrogant asshole. I just didn't know what was happening that night. I thought we had found a nice little rest house for diplomats and that they had room for us, a private room. And all it was . . . ugh. That was creepy.")

I'm glad we got ourselves out of there safely. I need to calm down; my mind is fuzzy, fighting nerves and lack of sleep. It seems that each day the intensity of our adventure ratchets up a notch or two. I worry what this day will bring. We are supposed to be going to Jerusalem. I should know what to expect, but now I'm unsure of myself. I'm not the expert traveller I thought I was. These biblical places have been a part of my life. Or should I say my fantasy, a dream of tiny buildings made of earth and straw dried in the sun, white flowing robes, gentle smiling bearded faces. The only thing that is true here for me is the desert, even though it is bigger, hotter, and emptier than I imagined.

We see a beaten-up sign indicating the Dead Sea is near-by. I am ecstatic. A civilized dip in the sea we've heard so much about in Sunday school should soothe and revive our souls. And there it is—a sea that is dead and a ramshackle resort on the shore that is also dead. It is spine-chilling and the strangeness engulfs me. Not to be defeated by disillusion-ment, for the record, we strip and go for a hot float.

When Marco Polo, his father, Nicolo, and uncle Maffeo arrived in Jerusalem about 1273, they were on a mission to fulfill a promise the elder Polos had made a few years before to Kublai Khan. They were to take oil from the Holy

Sepulchre at the base of the Mount of Olives near Jerusalem and bring it to him in China. It wasn't easy for Nicolo, Maffeo, and Marco. Jerusalem had been under siege for 2,000 years, as Romans, Christians, and much later Muslims vied for control. War and religious fervour were the only constants. And swarms of pilgrims. As soon as the Polos got the oil, they left.

When we arrived in Jerusalem in 1965, the Old City in the eastern part belonged to Jordan; the new city in the west belonged to Israel. The political situation was tenuous and, for the traveller, complicated.

We will not be able to enter Israel on this trip. If we cross over into the new part of Jerusalem, which is in Israel, we can't go back into the eastern, Jordanian, part to continue our trip. Fortunately, or should I say providentially, all the great Christian monuments I want to explore are on the Jordanian side. So are the swarms of tourists and pilgrims.

From our campsite near the Mount of Olives, I can see the golden cupola of the Dome of the Rock, built upon the Rock of Abraham, which is also said to be the rock from which the prophet Muhammad launched himself to take his place alongside Allah. A blend of Judaism, Christianity, and Islam, the Dome and its mosaic exterior were restored in 1964 with money from the Arab states.

When I step inside, I am awed by its simple elegance and feeling of peace.

That peace is shattered when I step out into the tourist shops lining Via Dolorosa and The Way of the Cross on the way to the Church of the Holy Sepulchre. Crammed inside the church are the leftovers of almost 2,000 years of tourists and pilgrims, and I have trouble believing the claim that this is the true site of Christ's crucifixion. The stories of my childhood, those of simple beauty, love, and compassion, are lost in this place.

Then we're off to Bethlehem or, in other words, away to the manger — Manger Square, Manger Street, Manger Café, and a heavenly host of Christmases.

The stories of my childhood and my dreams are shattered.

When Ross needed to return to Jerusalem in 2004 for business, I stayed home in Calgary. I didn't want to go, to face disappointment again. Then when he returned full of stories of its beauty — the Wall, the architecture, his hike out into the desert near Bethlehem to visit Saint Sabas's Monastery, his walk around Jericho — I was filled with envy.

Maybe I am equipped to handle the challenges
Of being a tourist,
Now. Forty-five years later.

I try to set aside my preconceptions
And settle in the place, to absorb what is there
Before my Own Eyes

Instead of depending on Others' Eyes.

I try to learn to say words in their language
And greet women and their children,
Shake their hands and smile.
Even play a game or two.

I try to be a chameleon,
And change as needed
Like Marco Polo did
With years of travel along the Silk Road.

VII

guns and lemons (IRAQ)

MARCO POLO WAS LOOKING for a way to bring silk back to Europe from China, but his travels did not go as planned. He finally returned to Italy twenty-four years later. His stories were sensational, and people had a hard time believing them. Then later, when he was thrown in jail for a few months, he met another prisoner who was a writer and was keen to help Marco get his stories written.

I think I know how Marco must have felt. Our trip didn't go as planned either, and for forty years I've been telling stories about our travels along the Silk Road. Now I'm trying to write about them. Some stories are more difficult to tell than others.

We are following ancient routes through the Middle East, routes early travellers like Alexander, Genghis Khan, and Marco Polo took. Jerusalem was not a safe place for Marco and his entourage, so they got out as quickly as they could.

We are in Jerusalem too and want to leave as soon as we can. But for different reasons. It's because Iraq is unsafe, and we want to get the ordeal we expect there over with as fast as possible. It won't be easy. International tension between Iraq and Western countries is significant, and there have been repeated military coups and countercoups. It is the only country for which, while we were in London, we were unable to obtain the visas, triptyques, and all the other papers we need to travel through the country.

Iraqis can't get visas into the West easily either.

Stories and rumours consume me. I dig out the guide-book and try to grasp what is going on and understand the animosity toward the West. The Treaty of Versailles, crafted by Western diplomats in 1919, reconfigured the Middle East. Great Britain, mandate holders in Iraq, decided that it should step back and create a monarchy. Faysal was crowned as the first king. After years of tension and change, in 1958 King Faysal was overthrown by a military coup. Between 1958 and now, 1965, there have been more coups and countercoups. Recently Saddam Hussein, the young renegade leader of the ousted Ba'ath Party, escaped prison and is on the loose. As a former interrogator and torturer, he is renowned for his ruthlessness.

I'm terrified, and Ross is bargaining with me to be reasonable.

"We can't listen to the stories and let this guy mess up our trip. We won't stop. We'll just drive straight across, and then we'll be in Iran where it's safe," he says.

I dig out the pamphlets we stashed in a door side pocket

of the Beetle and reread them. They tell me a story different from the terror in my imagination. I'm invited to visit beautiful, historic Mesopotamia, which is now Iraq. Mosul, Basra, Karbala, Babylon, and Baghdad are waiting for me.

A green and white pamphlet shows me a picture of a Venetian gondola skimming down a canal, and I read, "Come. Basra is the 'Venice of the East,' where the Tigris joins the Euphrates and where you will see the legendary spot of the Garden of Eden and Adam and Eve's apple tree."

Another has a sepia photo of an ancient, crumbling brick minaret. "Mosul is on the main route that links Iraq with Syria and Turkey and is where the ancient biblical city of Nineveh rests," I read.

The "holy city of Karbala is the resting place of Imam Al-Hussein, a grandson of the prophet Muhammad," a Shia martyr who was murdered there in AD 680 defending his faith.

Babylon, the ancient holy city of Mesopotamia, dates from 2300 BC. It is eighty kilometres from Baghdad and is where the Hanging Gardens of Babylon, one of the seven wonders of the ancient world, are said to be, the pamphlets go on. With grand gardens, opulent palaces, temples, and places of learning, it was the largest city in the world in 1770 BC.

My worries lose; Ross and the pamphlets win.

It is a long way to Iraq, and we want an early start into the uninhabited, forbidding black basalt Syrian Desert. We wake at 4:30 a.m. in Jerusalem, jump in the car, and drive away, chomping down our usual breakfast of hard-boiled eggs and bread and quaffing down a thermos of espresso.

We stop for more coffee in Amman. Are we procrastinating? The conversation is exciting, and we are enjoying other travellers' stories.

"And where are you going?" our fellow coffee shop travellers ask.

We tell them about Iraq. The pamphlet stories. I don't bother to tell them about the Saddam rumours and the coups.

"But haven't you heard? That place is very dangerous. Whatever you do, don't drive at night. Don't stop. You will be robbed for sure. And killed, probably."

I try to calm myself. "Of course we'll be safe. The pamphlets say so, more or less. We are poor. We have almost no money, no jewels, no guns, and no politics to peddle."

And so we set off across the desert at high noon. Off schedule and late.

The Beetle is bumping across the desert on a rough black basalt gravel road beside the Iraq Petroleum pipeline that goes across the desert to the Persian Gulf. This desert is different, bigger and more hostile than the Syrian Desert we crossed last week. Everything around me is flat, black, and shimmering under a gigantic fireball sun. The heat is unbearable. We get out the wet towels again and jam the windows closed. Our inspired air-conditioning system is not enough. It is too hot. I can't eat. I throw up. Nature's way to cool off, I suppose.

The sun. The heat. The parched, scorched earth. The thirst. There is nothing here. No water. No people. No robbers. Just me puking in the middle of nowhere.

Excitement? I am too weak to feel it.

What's that? Who is that? Fast approaching on the dark road behind us is a long black limousine. With Iraqi license plates. Everything is happening too fast—my heart, and the limo. The long car careens around our little Beetle, cuts us off, and in a cloud of sand, grinds to a stop.

Three big men wearing dark Western-style trousers and white dress shirts jump out and signal us to stop as they run around to the back of the limo. They yank open the trunk. We both shake uncontrollably and my stomach revolts against me. Again. I am paralysed with fear. Ross is speechless. For a change.

The trunk is filled with rifles. There is no body. Yet.

Silently, I try to calm myself. "Okay, Nancy, so this is how it's going to be. Oblivion. The end. I've always wondered what it would be like. But I'm taking the high road. I won't let that bastard know how I feel. I'll smile and wait for it to happen. No one will ever know how brave I was."

One of the men grabs the rifles.

And shoves them aside.

Then he grabs something from the trunk and walks toward us. He is carrying a small white bag.

"This is for you," he says gently. "We noticed that you were ill. These lemons will help."

The sun is sinking into the desert, and it is cooler now. Before we cross the Jordan customs control and the Iraqi frontier, we stop for a quick picnic, taking a chance that no thieves will confront us. It is peaceful here. I feel good, confident, buoyed by the kindness of the men in the limousine. We set up the picnic table in the sand beside the road and talk about our next stop.

Rutba. Rutba Wells. Wells? Water. An oasis.

I daydream of Mesopotamia, the ancient place that is now called Iraq and all the wells there. I see romantic, biblical visions of a latter-day spa.

"All of the flocks would gather there. The shepherds would roll the stone away from the well's opening. They would give water to the sheep. Then they would roll the stone back in its place over the opening of the well." Genesis 29:3.

I feel I have known Rutba Wells all my life. We will be there soon.

(I was so young then. Was I too trusting? Too "head in the clouds"? Whatever I was, I was on a steep learning curve, and my sense of security was soon to be trashed.)

The Rutba Wells of my starry-eyed expectations is a hellhole. There are colossal black, dirty trucks everywhere. Noisy, idling engines spew choking fumes and black, oily smoke. The bright orange and yellow Shell gas station, with searchlights that blaze high into the dark, casts a glow like a horror show.

And I am part of the show.

Hundreds of young men hang around. Most are in dark, dirty rags, some are in Western-style long pants and grubby collared shirts; others are bearded, wearing turbans and long, flowing Arabic robes. What are they doing? Waiting for work? It doesn't feel right for me to be here.

It is difficult not to be noticed, with my short-cropped bare head and pink face. I feel naked. I do not see another woman. I try to quietly slip into nobody-ness. Do not talk, Nancy. Don't look. Bow your head and follow. They will not see me.

Ross takes the lead and I am invisible.

I shove. I scream and I run when the horrible man grabs me as I come out of the "ladies" washroom behind the gas station. I hit him hard. I run and I scream. Ross comes running, yelling. The gas station boss comes running too, with a look of terror. I shout. I cry.

Ross smashes his fist on the wall and hollers at the boss man, at everyone. "What the hell is going on in this place? You dirty swine."

Two worried-looking men come toward us, dragging the assailant by his ears. A crowd gathers.

"Get them away from us," Ross shouts at the boss. Then he turns and yells at me. "We're getting out of here. Now. Fast."

And so we begin the long drive through the scary night to Baghdad.

We arrive in Baghdad about 6:00 a.m., August 14, 1965.

(Is it a coincidence that Baghdad is on my mind now, almost half a century later? Were there signs then of the deadly role Iraq would play in today's "war against terror"?)

The empty campground we find ourselves in is beside the Tigris River, which circles Baghdad with its twin, the Euphrates. Graceful, cool-looking date palms shade the grounds, and little grass-roofed picnic shelters dot the riverbank. There is an eerie quietness. The grounds are spotless.

It is very hot. We are exhausted, and we can do nothing but crawl into our tent and sleep.

We wake at noon.

A pleasant-looking, clean-shaven young man dressed in Western-style trousers and a white short-sleeve cotton shirt ambles over to our tent to greet us. "Most of Baghdad is asleep. It is too hot to be awake," he says. "This is the week the dates turn from green to brown in Baghdad."

Soon, friends he has invited come to meet us. They look at us curiously, seeming to say, "Who are these strange people who travel across the desert to Baghdad in August? They must be a hardy variety of people."

We sit at the picnic tables under the date palms, drink tea, and talk about the world and about Canada and Iraq.

They tell us about the Hanging Gardens of Babylon and the great arch at Ctesiphon. "They are close by. Perhaps this is why you have come to Baghdad? We will take you there."

"We should go. We're lucky to have them offer to guide us. They're so proud of their history," Ross says.

"I can't go. I'm exhausted. I just want to be still and rest. You go. I'll stay here and wait. I'm so tired. These guys are nice, but this whole country is scary. Even the heat is scary," I plead.

"You're right. We should move on. We'll get up early and leave in the morning. Maybe we can come back."

It hurts to remember how disappointed our Baghdad

friends were that we left.

I wish I could tell them that I'm sorry we changed our plans and didn't get to Babylon.

Saddam Hussein started building on top of it in 1983, restoring some parts. He had his name inscribed all over the new bricks. He was building a cable car over the city when the Americans invaded Iraq in 2003.

Atop the ruins of Babylon, the Americans built a huge helipad and a large parking lot for heavy equipment. The helicopter landings caused many of the ruins underneath to collapse, and 4,000 years of history were buried.

What happened to the young caretaker and his pals who befriended us in the campsite and the kind men with the rifles in the car trunk? I sit here at my computer and try to piece together what their story might be. How does their story fit into what I find?

BBC News, September 3, 2007. Iraq War timeline. British prime minister dismisses the suggestion that the pullout of 5,500 British troops from the palace at Basra is a defeat.

CBC special news coverage, October 11, 2007, reporting for September 2007. Two million Iraqis are displaced and two million Iraqis have fled the country. Most Iraqis consider their police corrupt and murderous.

Washington Post, January 9, 2008. According to the World Health Organization and the Iraqi government, 151,000 Iraqis were killed between March 2003 and June 2006, the three years after the United States invaded.

January 10, 2008. In the span of ten minutes, American warplanes dropped as many explosives as they usually do in a month, a thundering barrage of more than 40,000 pounds of bombs intended to blow up stashes of insurgent weapons.

OUR
CAMPSITE
IN BAGHDAD

persepolis

VIII

redefining iran

MARCO POLO CROSSED PERSIA twice—once on his way to China and once twenty years later on his way back home to Venice. We also crossed Persia twice, only our trips were three months apart, 690 years after Marco Polo's.

The savvy Rusticello, Marco's fellow prisoner, realized that Marco's colourful stories could be the opportunity of a lifetime for a writer. The collaboration that resulted produced a book that shook Europeans' notions of what Central Asia and China were like.

Now I'm trying to write a book about what it was like for me to travel along the Silk Road. I wish I had Marco's talent for remembering and embellishment or a magic pen that would help me put it all down on paper. Today I'm supposed to be working on my Iran chapter, but really I have no idea how to define my experience there. My story is so far away, lost for forty-odd years in the depths of the grey, solid mass that is my brain. I know it's in there somewhere, though. The memories.

I force myself to sit down and put my pencil on the page. I bought a new pencil yesterday, a pretty one, to see if it would help rev up my memory, like turning the key in my car. I tell myself it's good to go for a ride, to remember. "It's decent physical exercise, Nancy. The whatevers in the brain charge up sooner or later, once the glow plug ignites them."

I begin by writing down unconnected fragments of what I remember, and I make a list—a woman in a black chador is gliding past an immense blue-and-gold-tiled mosque; the Beetle is chugging along a corrugated dirt road, leaving behind a tunnel of sand; I drink tea in tiny glass vessels with women who cannot speak my language. I search for the connections, the detail in between the words on my list. I reread letters I sent our mothers. They're fragmented, selected pieces of information carefully chosen to let them know how happy and safe I am—the kind of letter well known to many travellers who write from afar to assuage their moms' worry.

I read my travel journals again and again looking for words that are not there but hidden in the depths of my mind. At least there's a map in the back pages and a title I wrote for each day's note, like "Abdeh to Yazd." But it's still as though I've never been there before.

I Google. I Wikipedia.

I read books about Gertrude Bell, Freya Stark, and other women who are models of independent adventure. My stories are different from theirs because there is an over-powering element of "we" in my account that is difficult to separate from the "I."

I look through old photographs. I interview Ross. Ah. His words ignite my remembering. My heart begins to thump more quickly. I am almost there.

I go to the kitchen for a glass of water before I try another start. I open the pantry door and see, hidden in the corner, the hand-hammered copper bowl. Ross bought that bowl in Kerman in eastern Iran, at the bazaar, from a grizzled, smiling coppersmith who could not understand why Ross would buy it before it was polished smooth. Ross said he wanted it rough and hammered so he could touch the man's real work, not an indifferent, machine-polished, perfect piece like the other polished bowls in the souk. Now I too can feel the handwork and am on my way to telling you what it was like for me when we crossed Iran twice that year.

It is August 15. We are glad to be rid of Iraq. The border crossing was chaotic, as they usually are for us these days. Hundreds of Persian and Iraqi women, children, and men lingered behind the barbed wire fences, stopped in their tracks by guards. A cholera epidemic is spreading into Iran, and people are being quarantined at the frontiers. They have been waiting to cross the border for five days.

We are relieved the soldiers finally let us go through after taking three hours to check our documents. I feel safe now that we're in Iran, on our way to Kermanshah, a town close to the Iraqi border. It's early evening, and we feel free as the Beetle roars over cool, rolling foothills on a good paved road. Am I dreaming? Am I really on the route Marco Polo described? Forever, this land, with its high mountains and fertile valleys, has defined the roads people take and the places people live.

Stunning mountain peaks surround Kermanshah and seem to call us to hike them. So we stop for a few moments to take in the fresh air and the view. We won't be able to hike here this time; we need a good night's sleep before driving on to Tehran.

Our hotel is comfortable, with a welcoming, geranium-filled inner courtyard. People drift in and out. Most women are wearing long black cloaks — all but their eyes and feet covered — that give me a comfortable feeling. I know I am somewhere both exotic and defiant. The former shah banned the chador years ago with his program for modernizing Iran. Are the veiled women in Kermanshah bucking the rule?

Shah Mohammad Reza Pahlavi, the present shah, is young, forty-five years old, and his life, for me, is a fairy tale. He claims to be descended from Darius the Great, hero of Persia, who ruled 1,500 years ago. Darius was noted for administrative and legal reforms, and so is the shah.

He was educated in Swiss boarding schools and in a military academy in Tehran. His wife (his third) is two years older than I am, studied architecture in Paris, and is famously beautiful.

Now the fairy tale ends.

We are told that the shah has absolute control over all Iran. Democracy appears to be unknown in this part of the world. And that worries me. I ask myself, "So why is the shah a darling of Western democracies like Canada and the United States? How can it be?"

⌛

Forty years have given me time to think about what's happened in Iran. Would world politics have taken a different course if people like me had spoken up and had tried harder to find answers to our questions?

I review the facts as I see them. Iran was officially neutral during World War I, but when its close neighbour, Turkey, aligned with Germany, Britain got worried. So it barged in and occupied large parts of Iran to protect its own oil interests. After the war, Reza Khan, a brilliant, well-liked military officer, backed a coup d'etat that obstructed Britain's control. He became the first shah of the Pahlavi dynasty in 1925, and his goal was to modernize and transform Iran into an industrial, urbanized country.

Britain, however, retained control of all oil resources and the Anglo-Iranian Oil Company. This became especially problematic in 1939, at the beginning of World War II. Shah Reza Khan proclaimed Iran to be neutral once again. In 1941 the British insisted that Iran was harbouring German spies. They demanded that the shah deport all German citizens living there. The shah refused, so Britain and its friend Russia invaded the country and sent him into exile in September of that year.

A year or so later the Russian forces, who had their hands full in Europe, left Iran, and the United States filled the gap by sending in a military force to maintain a new railway line for transporting oil to the Persian Gulf.

I have trouble figuring out why, after the Brits threw out Shah Reza Khan, they put his twenty-one-year-old son, Mohammed Reza Pahlavi, on the throne, but they did. Now in 2008, with the benefit of history, the answers are becoming clearer to me.

It's all about oil. Power is oil; oil is power.

In 1951 Dr. Mohammed Mossadegh became the first (and, as a matter of fact, the only) truly democratically elected prime minister in Iran. He won by a huge majority. His focus was to nationalize Iran's oil industry. Of course, the British didn't like that, so they colluded with the United States. In a CIA-orchestrated coup d'etat, the passionate nationalist Mossadegh was arrested and remained under house arrest, out of the way of imperialism for the rest of his life, but his legacy as champion of third-world anti-imperialism endures today.

It is 1965, and as we travel around Iran we see that Americans have a powerful influence. The friendly Shah Mohammed Reza Pahlavi, with the help of the United States and the influence of his progressive father, is changing Iran, a country whose values are traditionally conservative, Muslim, and rural. I'm thrilled to be able to see for myself the shah's efforts — women are becoming freer of restrictive Muslim law; a strong program of industrialization,

especially in the oil sector, is bringing Iran into the twentieth century.

Iran is getting rich. So is the shah.

It surprises me that anyone would dare assassinate
him, but there have been two attempts on his life, one by
a religious fundamentalist, about fifteen years ago, and
another by a soldier who shot his way into the shah's palace
four months ago.

(Ah! I was innocent then, trapped by Western propaganda. Everything was too perfect—too perfect to be true.
Shah Mohammed Reza was a scoundrel.

Could I have known then that something was askew?
What are the real facts? And what is not real? I ask more
questions now.

After a few years in the late 1970s the people of Iran
were fed up with the shah—his iron rule, his reforms, his
lavish lifestyle, and his love affair with the Americans. There
were riots, strikes, and mass demonstrations. Eventually,
Shah Mohammed Reza Pahlavi and his family were forced
out of the country. People embraced an exiled Islamic
fundamentalist cleric called Ayatollah Ruholla Khomeini,
who returned from exile in Paris to cheering crowds in Iran.
He held a referendum, proclaimed a new Islamic Republic
of Iran, and threw out the Americans.)

We drive through rich, fertile plains into Tehran: the
Atlantic Hotel and the first bath I've had since Venice. We
spend the next morning at the Museum of Archaeology
soaking up its messages, from the time of Darius, in bas-
relief, pottery, and ancient columns. It is noon when we

leave, and outside the concrete-and-asphalt city is burning hot in the intense sun.

We make a snap decision to escape to the beaches. Noshahr, on the Caspian Sea, is the summer capital of Tehran and is where the shah's summer residence is.

A modern, attractively landscaped highway between 4,500-metre mountains and across the spectacular new Karaj Dam is cool and fast. As we descend the other side of the pass, the climate changes. For the first time since we left Europe, it's raining, and the vegetation is tropical, lush, and green.

We drive by several inviting motels along the Caspian coast and stop at a small palm-fringed compound near a beach. Chickens run around the rose gardens and playground, some children play soccer, and smaller ones ride swings and seesaws. Adults mingle and speak in muffled tones on green lawns in the humid evening air.

There's a restaurant in a garden beside the sea; gentle waves lap the shore, and several grass-roofed platforms with mats for overnight visitors dot the grounds.

We're hungry, and the staff is keen to cook dinner for us.

"Our specialty is chicken kebab, rice, and salad," the owner says with a big smile. A little group of friendly onlookers gathers around, eager to help us choose our menu. They don't see many foreign visitors here.

Soon several little boys are running around the yard chasing a chicken. A few minutes later we hear a bloody squawk.

When our barbecued chicken arrives, I have lost my appetite.

The night on the platform with the grass roof is long. Kids are screaming, waves thunder, and chickens screech. Finally I fall asleep but wake with my own screech.

"What's happening?" I yell. "Something's attacking. Get up, get up."

Chickens flap and squawk frantically under our platform.

Ross mumbles, "No. Nothing's happening. Nobody's trying to rob us. It's a dog. A hungry dog. Looking for chickens."

A man hollers. The dog runs away, and quiet, except for the sound of the sea, fills the night.

I am happy to be back in my elegant Hotel Atlantic in Tehran, $5.30 a night with breakfast and my own bathtub. "Tehran is like the Continental Divide, the place where the hotels are cheaper than the campsite," I write my mother, "and where the West confronts the East."

"Tehran was the most sophisticated city we'd been in since Beirut," Ross said when I asked him the other day to help me remember. "It was a nice feeling being there. It was progressive, full of hope, a future to look forward to."

The streets were green, lined with big trees. People wore Western clothes, mostly. They filled the sidewalks in the evening, promenading along the boulevards, talking and taking in the fresh night air. There was a beautiful hill in the city and we walked up it, to the new Hilton Hotel.

"Remember those exquisite silver shot glasses with the

turquoise inlay?" Ross asked. They were in a little shop near the hotel. And we couldn't buy them because they were too expensive for us. About $6 each. Ross will never let me forget what we left behind in Iran. And he's right. It's important to remember what it was like for us.

I have photographs, letters we sent, and my journal—my lists—that tell of our stroll around the iron gates of the forbidden Golestan Palace and its rose gardens that beckoned us to come in closer; the shah's former summer residence with its eighteen opulent palaces and fabulous gardens; and Sepahsalar Mosque, one of the most note-worthy examples of Persian architecture in the world, with famous poetry inscribed in its tiles.

I can still smell the market and rows of rice sold there. It's curious. Sometimes I think I can't remember anything, and then this peculiar feeling comes, and I think I'm there again.

I want to know these people who are walking beside me. We smile and nod. I can speak just two words they'll understand. *Salaam aleikum.* I can't read the newspaper or understand the radio. There is no TV. I hear angry, rough voices gathering down the street, but the sweet faces of people walking with me tell me that they want to be friends. I don't know what's going on. So I don't worry.

Maybe I should have tried harder then to understand.

When we returned to Tehran, later that year, on our way back to Europe, we didn't go into the city centre. Instead we camped in the middle of the city's main roundabout on the outskirts of town.

Two Swiss adventurers and their entourage were there. They were also following Marco Polo's route, but they were on camels, filming their story for *National Geographic*. A confusion of animals, grubby bearded travellers, local Iranian news reporters, tents, clothes hanging on lines, and tea steaming on sputtering camp stoves crowded the small patch of grass that was our campsite. Cars and trucks blasted their way around the cloverleaf. Delicious Iranian butter sugar cookies were passed with tea, and we shared our stories, a ritual travellers know well. The Swiss adventurers said they should write about us. I said, "Thanks, but we'll write our own someday."

I didn't know it would take me another forty-five years to put my stories down on paper.

Journal entry, August 20, 1965. "Flat, arid, beautiful. The desert is becoming almost like home now. We are excited to be travelling on and to leave the sophistication of Tehran behind. We pass simple brown-walled villages on the road toward Shiraz, Isfahan, and Persepolis."

An abandoned collection of sandstone monuments emerges in the distance through haze and swirling dust devils, and the ancient palaces of Darius the Great make themselves known to us.

It is Persepolis—immense and magnificent. "Nobody had ever told me how beautiful it was going to be," Ross says in a soft, reverent voice. "Why didn't I learn about this place in school?"

Alone, we stroll through giant columns and colossal buildings while sand swirls around, transporting me into another world.

"How could I have missed the significance of what Darius did for his empire, before the Greeks came?" asks Ross.

The remains of ramparts, ceremonial staircases, water towers, and a sewage system help us fill the gaps in the story we know of Darius's gift to his people. Two thousand years later, the sculptural art form of bas-reliefs, depicting Darius's guests from all over the Persian Empire, bearing him gifts, helps me look into the hearts and minds of people who lived then. Bulls, lions, eagles of grey marble tell me the tale of a push for power.

(In 1971, to celebrate 2,500 years since the founding of the Persian monarchy by Darius, Shah Reza Pahlavi held one of the most lavish parties the world had ever seen at Persepolis. His extravagance, geared toward impressing the West, did not sit well with the Iranian public, who were mainly conservative Muslims. The big party at Persepolis was probably the beginning of the end of the monarchy, once and for all.)

It is evening in Isfahan. I'm standing beside the Masjed-e-Shah Mosque with its massive minarets and double-layered dome covered with luminescent blue tiles sparkling and shifting colour.

"This extraordinary artistic endeavour was the best that society produced hundreds of years ago, and you can see how it has stood the test of time," Ross explains as we walk around the plaza. Sunlight continually changes the beauty of curved lines, delicate patterns, and breathtaking colours in the tiling. I am oblivious to all else. This mosque is mine, built for me, to inspire, to enlighten, and to calm me.

That night, we met some Americans our age working with the Peace Corps. We were happy to have their company, and we stayed up late to eat cookies from the local bakery, watch movies, and drink beer. Again I was caught in our comfortable, shallow world.

In Isfahan, the Masjed-e-Shah is now known as Masjed-e-Imam, because imams, religious leaders, replaced the shahs as rulers of Iran in 1979 when Shah Mohammed Reza Pahlavi left. His programme of westernization and industrialization had failed. It met with solid resistance from the majority of people in Iran. Massive demonstrations became violent when they faced the shah's brutal military.

Adoring millions greeted Ayatollah Khomeini when he returned from exile to take control of Iran. Little did his adoring millions realize that Khomeini's brand of Islamic fundamentalism and nationalism meant he would change Iran, with brutal efficiency, to set up an imam-dominated

Islamic republic.

The fact that the imams renamed my beloved Masjed-e-Shah to Masjed-e-Imam Mosque pales beside the disappearances and executions that took place in Iran as minor officials in the new regime took the law into their own hands. Hatred against the United Sates and Israel, who had supported the shah, was encouraged and grew.

In November 1979 Islamic militants imprisoned fifty-two American hostages inside the U.S. Embassy in Tehran. We all followed the daily news. Six American diplomats evaded capture and ran to the Canadian Embassy.

In September 1980 Iraq's Saddam Hussein tried to grab Iran's oil, and a war broke out between the two countries that lasted eight years.

In the mid-nineties we decided it was time for us to return to Iran, to learn more about the kind and hospitable people we knew lived there. We would go by foot this time, hike up into the mountains with a guide and an interpreter. We made the arrangements.

Our guides e-mailed me, saying I would need to wear a chador. "To wear? Hiking? A chador?" I asked.

"Yes," they said, and the reality of what was happening in Iran took hold. We decided to wait for a better time to go.

It is June 2009, and we are here in Paris to celebrate our forty-fifth wedding anniversary. I've been thinking a lot about that first time we travelled together along the Silk

Road. Iran is in the news again, and I'm trying to redefine it for myself, given what's been happening. Forty-four years ago on a sunny hot day, like it is today, we were in Tehran. A lot has changed since. Today I couldn't wear a short skirt there like I did forty-four years ago. Rules for women mean that now I would have to cover up and be segregated from men in most restaurants and other public places.

The world expects an eruption of violence in Iran any day now. Its nuclear capability is a special concern. The June 12 election this year was determined illegal by the opposition parties, caused riots all over Iran, and put 2,000 people in jail. Nonetheless, President Ahmadinejad was returned to power. Western countries are outraged. Here in France, the home of Liberty, Equality, and Fraternity, people are especially active in their fury.

The Paris Metro is packed, but I've learned to use my greying hair and wrinkles to advantage, and as the train starts moving, the other passengers clear a path for me. I lurch toward an empty seat beside the door. The guy beside me seems innocuous enough, but Ross, who is doing his own lurching and swaying in the crowd, is looking at me strangely, and I sense that he means me to beware. I admit the guy beside me gives me the creeps, though I don't know why. He's dressed decently enough. He has a slim build, with an intense Aryan face and a motley, rough beard. His dark eyes dart around the squealing subway car as it scrapes its way at high speed along metal tracks. He scans the crowd, then stares at the door. Abruptly he turns his head to the black window beside him and fearfully fixes his eyes out into the dark tunnel. Suddenly, but purposefully, he pulls from his pocket a small white plastic box with two switches on it, one black and one red. He looks toward the crowd and presses the red button. The subway screeches to a stop, the doors open, and I stagger toward Ross and push him out the door.

"Let's go. Faster. That guy is freaking me out."

"Don't worry. I was watching him," Ross says, stumbling over the crowded platform, "and then I decided his therapist probably told him to click that thing every time he got scared."

"You always think the best. I thought he was an Iranian terrorist about to blow us up."

"It was very strange, but you notice the Parisians didn't seem to worry."

We are hot and exhausted and decide to sit for a while in the plaza beside the wild and colourful Georges Pompidou Centre to take in the excitement of the summer solstice. Everyone, it seems, is here — the mime artists, the comedians, the musicians, the dancers, the children. The whirl of a festive-looking helicopter making tight circles overhead drowns out the music, and then the immense yellow, red, and black machine pauses, hanging in midair. We wait with happy expectation.

"Look. The French are fabulous. Even the helicopter matches the Tingly sculpture over there. There's going to be a spectacle. Someone's going to parachute down into the square. Some acrobats," Ross remarks.

"Nah. They couldn't. There are too many people here.

It's a heli tour," I tell him.

Bang. A loud explosion rocks the square.

"What happened?" I ask. "A bomb? People are running."

A huge cloud of black smoke fills the far corner of the square, exactly where we ate our lunch watching the kids play.

"We need to get out of here, fast."

We take off running into a quiet alley, quickly check the map for a way out, and walk toward a main street. The wail of French police sirens comes closer and closer. The helicopter circles get tighter. Just before we are to emerge onto the main street, a fleet of twenty police buses arrives, blocking the exit. Everyone is running. I want to run home, but for now I'll try to duck into this café. The staff is locking the door. Now it's closed. I yell to Ross who's several metres behind to get the hell over here.

He says, "Wait, we have to figure out what to do."

I think, "I'm too old to be in another James Bond movie. Let's just move. Anywhere but here." But Ross is more rational.

A sleek body in black pushes through the crowd. Its head, covered in a tight black hood except for a stark white mask covering its face, stretches up like a periscope, peers around, and ducks.

Columns of gendarmes advance behind us, batons drawn and shields up. I'm terrified. The masked black body slinks down into the crowd, out of sight. Ross and I press ourselves against a wall while the police advance, ignore us, and squeeze themselves deeper into the crowd, batons ready.

I'm free now and can breathe. Now it's time for us to run.

When we get back to the hotel a half hour later, I Google "Paris demonstrations." One site asks for our photos of it. Another tells us that there are protests in Paris to support Iranian citizens who dispute their country's corrupt election results.

My story about Iran is redefined but is endless.

shiraz

crossing the desert again

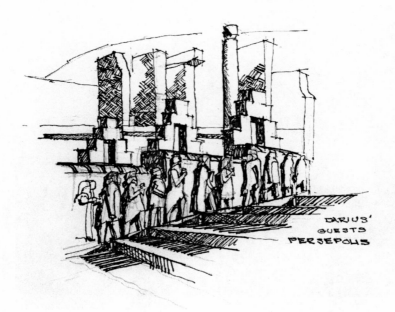

musician in ghazi stadium, kabul, 1965

IX

pulling away but wanting to stay
(IRAN TO AFGHANISTAN)

A feeling of awe mixes with my anxiety as we bump through rock and gravel ravines, sneak around sinkholes, and marvel at some of the tallest dunes in the world. I feel as though we will never get to Afghanistan, where we will stop and rest for a few days before we travel on through the Khyber Pass to Pakistan and then finally to India.

This desert in Iran, the Dasht-e-lut, covers 20,000 square miles.

Hello? Why isn't anyone here?

We've driven 235 miles today and have seen two trucks and one bus in the ten hours it's taken us. I've read that sometimes the surface temperatures reach 159 degrees Fahrenheit. I haven't checked, but maybe today is one of those sometimes. No wonder no one's here.

We need to find a safe place to stop. As night closes in, a pretty adobe settlement breaks through the blandness of the desert. It is Yazd, the oldest inhabited city in Iran and a centre for the Zoroastrian faith, in which the belief is in the purity of the elements — earth, water, and fire. On nearby hills, the dead are left exposed on top of Towers of Silence, where vultures clean them off so the corpses won't pollute the earth.

Fire is the Zoroastrian symbol of god, and we try to get a glimpse inside the main temple here, where a perpetual fire burns. I feel uncomfortable in this place, and a sinister-looking guard wearing a dark cloak is clearly not comfortable with my being here. Wagging his turbaned head furiously, he charges toward us and shooes us away from the sacred territory he protects.

No worries. I'm happy to spend the rest of the evening sitting in the pretty courtyard of our guesthouse reviewing our travel plan. We will forge through the endless desert for two more days. On the way we'll stop in Kerman and Zahedan, then we'll cross the Iranian border into Pakistan for one night in Quetta before we head north and cross the Afghan border.

Journal entry, August 28, 1965. "We drive through rugged clumps of the Suleiman Mountains that simply rise out of the desert, then across a flat, fertile plain to Kandahar. Fields of brilliant purple strawflowers mingle with luscious orchards of sweet fruit, apricots, and pomegranates, for which this area is famous. A tree-lined American-built road passes a new international airport and leads to a scruffy city centre with a shabby hotel, another pretty courtyard, and

94

regal Afghan carpets."

The fields and orchards in the countryside remind me of home.

We drive onward to Kabul along a new paved highway through green valleys flanked by the Hindu Kush mountains. Evening sun, like a giant orange, shines through a fine mist. I'm in awe of Afghanistan's beauty.

Kabul is large and busy. Turbaned and cloaked descendants of Babur, Genghis Khan, and Alexander the Great crowd the streets alongside Americans and Europeans in Western dress. The bazaar is alive with colour, intrigue, and everything anyone could need, including the Afghan carpets I covet. At the Khyber Restaurant in the centre of town, where the music is too loud but cheerful and familiar, we gobble up European food, scrumptious steaks and fresh vegetables, the first we've had in weeks. We enjoy meeting other travellers, who, like Marco Polo, delight in embellishing their travel adventures.

"Be sure to go to the festivities at the stadium," someone tells us. "It's the Pashtunistan Day celebrations."

We tag along with some photographers from *National Geographic* and are caught up in the excitement at Ghazi Stadium. Spirited music is performed on exotic horns. Thousands of spectators cheer on a rousing match of *buzkashi*, a sort of Afghan polo played with a goat carcass, and other games of endurance and strength. Later, to calm down, cool down, and immerse ourselves in Afghan history, we stroll through a peaceful park built 450 years ago as a place for public recreation and as the final resting place of the first Mogul emperor, Babur.

It is a whirlwind tour of Afghanistan and we love it. We want to see as much as we can before we have to leave, so we settle for a drive north of Kabul into the mountains. We've arranged to go with a Polish family recently transferred to Kabul from the USSR. They have a Beetle just like ours, and we go in tandem. For security.

We forget the omnipresent politics of the day. And the wars. We are happy and confident in our travel prowess.

I have nightmares now knowing that Ghazi Stadium was the site of horrific public executions by the Taliban government in Afghanistan thirty years later, in the 1990s.

Perhaps if we had thought more about it, we would have turned back home then.

But we didn't. After a week of treasured experience in a country that we didn't want to leave, we began to pull ourselves away. Forever.

Or so we thought.

X

the khyber pass

*T*he Khyber Pass was an important link for many invaders and travellers throughout history, but Marco Polo was not one of them. He took a northern route across Afghanistan to get to China. We are going to follow the challenging route Alexander the Great set out on in 326 BC, when he left Afghanistan and crossed the pass into South Asia to conquer the Indus Valley. It is also the route Timur and Babur took.

"Khyber" in the Persian language means "high fort." Arid mountains tower above the pass, a narrow slit in the Hindu Kush mountain range. Our British Automobile Association (BAA) guidebook notes that the highway is paved and in good condition, although it is in a tribal area and "the local government has little authority." BAA recommends caution. Smuggling and kidnappings are common.

September 5, 1965. I'm eager to get on the road again. The dramatic history and geographical importance of the Khyber have piqued my imagination. We take down our camp beside the Khyber Dam on the outskirts of Kabul, eat a decent breakfast of imitation bacon and fried eggs at the Khyber Restaurant, and then head for the bazaar. Before we go, we need to change our money into Pakistani rupees.

The exchange rate for rupees is volatile, and we've heard a rumour that it's forbidden to bring them into Pakistan. To be safe, we hide them in the door panel of the Beetle.

We have enough money left over in our budget to buy sheepskin coats, and new shock absorbers for the Beetle were installed and paid for yesterday. The coat seller is waiting for us. We know him well because we looked at his beautiful handmade coats and drank tea with him yesterday.

Jasper got hold of my Afghan coat years ago and chewed it to bits. He heard me screaming in horror when I discovered his path of destruction, so he plunked his sixty-pound body down flat on the floor and looked up at me with those sweet brown eyes of his. "It's not my fault," he seemed to be telling me. "I'm trying to be a good puppy. But that fine sheepskin is just too tasty."

I couldn't throw out the coat, and bits of it hang in the basement cupboard now. My shredded Afghan coat is still beautiful, with its tender, pale-brown suede, delicately embroidered in swirls of soft green silk, and its lining of pure cream sheep's wool. When I got back to Montreal that cold winter of 1966, I would wrap it around my great belly before I went outside. It was a warm, cosy feeling, and I would think about Afghanistan—the memories were much fresher then. Whether I was riding the crowded bus down Rue Guy or climbing through snow on Sherbrooke Street, the coat and my big belly spurred conversation.

There's a lot we don't understand. People have told us that fighting between India and Pakistan in Kashmir has escalated. The dispute, over whose territory it is, has been going on for years, but now our dream of sitting in the sunshine on the deck of a houseboat in Kashmir for a few days, before we go on to Delhi, has been squashed.

"We can't go near Kashmir," Ross says, examining the map. "We'll just head for the Taj Mahal, south of Delhi. We'll be there in three days. It'll be okay that way. Remember, people speak English. In fact, they're almost British; they drive on the left-hand side of the road."

We drive south from Kabul and descend steeply through the Lataband Pass into a checkerboard valley of green vineyards bordered by tall poplars. Misty-blue mountains surround the valley. We go through Jalalabad. This is where the big juicy green grapes we saw in the market come from. We should be at the border crossing in an hour.

The mountains cast a dark, cold shade on the road, and we are getting more anxious about customs control. We pass through Afghan customs at Dakka and drive onto a narrow, newly paved road toward the Pakistani customs. The stashed rupees are on my mind, and I'm worried. "They'll figure we're hiding something. I'm nervous. They'll see it on my face."

We stop. I suppose this is the border. There is a man sitting on the front porch of a bungalow. He doesn't have a uniform on, but from the deferential treatment he's receiving from neat, professional-looking soldiers, we realize he's important, even though he's dressed in baggy blue pyjamas. He slowly gets up, saunters over to our car, and pokes his head in beside Ross's. With a sneer, he says in confident, but difficult-to-understand, English, "I want to ask you, what is this dahting?"

Ross's face blanches. "I don't understand. What do you mean by *dahting*?"

"Get out. Come to my office," the boss man says, opening our car door and beckoning Ross to follow him.

Escape plans — escape-from-jail plans — race through my head as I sit inside and watch the man's excitable manner as he questions Ross. Ross is quiet, serious, and thoughtful looking. Now Ross is talking. What is he saying? The man looks relieved, smiles, shakes Ross's hand, and escorts him back to the car. Ross says goodbye, and without a pause puts the key in the ignition and drives straight through customs toward the Khyber Pass.

"He wanted to know what dating was," Ross says.

"What do you mean, *dating*?"

"You know, when a boy asks a girl for a date. They don't

100

do that here. They don't understand. This might be the first time they've seen a boy and a girl travelling together."

"We may be a boy and a girl, but this isn't exactly a date. Did you tell him that?"

I take a deep breath and settle into the delights of driving through the Khyber Pass. The sun is setting and casts a blanket of gold on the high red sandstone cliffs that surround us. We drive into darkness and can only imagine the forts and the ghosts of history in this pass. It is very quiet and peaceful. The road is good. In an hour or so we will be in Peshawar.

Suddenly, quiet turns to deafening blaring as an enormous truck comes toward us. Its lights blind. The horn blasts again and again. Help me. I am on the right side of the road. Right, right? No, left. Right is wrong. Left is right. Left in Pakistan. We are in Pakistan. Brakes screech. Tires squeal. Turn, Nancy. Stay on the road. Stay away from the truck. The truck swerves. We are hopeless fools. But safe.

It is September 6, 1965. We arrived in Peshawar last night. The city stinks of sewage, diesel, rotten food, and other dying things. The only place we could find to stay is a dirty, noisy, crowded one-story hotel built around an open courtyard. We lived the chaos around us all night. From silent looks and tired faces, it seems no one else could sleep either.

The egg sandwiches we ordered for supper had dirty fingerprints on them. They did not go down well, and the big lump in my stomach lets me know that the sandwiches are still there. But the sun is shining already, the temperature is fine, and in a few hours we'll be in Lahore, near the Indian border.

Strangely, in Pakistan, there is an air of civilization that we understand. There are newspapers, and a local radio station blares out the news on our car radio. Lots of news. In Urdu. It feels good to hear news, even though we can't understand a word.

As we approach the outskirts of Lahore, people carrying big bundles walk, run, and bicycle toward us, crowding the shoulders of the busy road. Cars, trucks, tractors, and animals are everywhere. We inch our way along.

"Why are so many people leaving? Is it a holiday, like Pashtunistan Day in Afghanistan?"

"I guess so. They seem to have a lot of holidays in this part of the world," Ross says with a catch in his voice, as he veers around obstructions on the highway.

"By the way, what are those big machines in the ditch for?" I ask.

"Those are antiaircraft guns."

"What are antiaircraft guns?"

"They're for shooting down planes."

I am impressed. "How do you know that?"

"From summers in the navy."

I guess his summers as a student in the navy taught him something. I drop the subject.

(What was going on in Ross's head, I didn't know then. This side of the Khyber Pass was supposed to be like home. It did not occur to me that the world I was in could be at war. But Ross knew.)

I can't wait to pick up the mail at the American Express office. We haven't had a letter for weeks, and I can barely contain my excitement, although there is a strange quiet on the street—in fact, it is deserted. It must be a holiday. There is the front door. It has a note nailed on it. I dash over to read it. "Oh no. It's closed. Oh no. No. It says it's closed until further notice." Lahore is being evacuated.

September 6 marked the official beginning of the Indo-Pakistani war of 1965, when the Indian Army battled through the Pakistan border to within range of the Lahore airport. It is now celebrated as Defence Day every year in Pakistan.

evacuating lahore, 1965

XI

real/not real
(GETTING OUT OF PAKISTAN)

"SO IF THE CITY is evacuated, how come we're here?"
I ask.

Distant rumblings in the dark evening are like thunder,
except that the noise is too regular, too patterned, and too
decisive. Decisively deadly. The city is quiet, organized,
and empty. Several men in suits, not uniformed but official
looking, carry gallon paint cans and brushes. Purposefully,
they run around the streets quietly giving orders, blowing
muffled whistles. One of them paints our headlights black.
He waves us on, indicating we must get out of the way.

Away? I am trapped in a world I do not know. Is this
war?

War: noun. Conflict and killing between two countries.
An indistinct concept is becoming real for me. As in the calm
before a storm, I struggle for control and begin to accept
the new reality. I feel weird. I should be hysterical, but I am
oddly composed, focused, and sure of myself. Ross and I

105

are transformed into a solid, close-knit team. We will break through the wall of resistance and get out of Lahore. Fast. But how? It's dark. We have no gas and no headlights. We're tired. We're hungry.

"Okay. We need time to think and work out how we can get back to the border," Ross says. "But first we have to find a safe place for us to stay tonight and get some sleep."

"This is an emergency. We need a phone right away to call the Canadian embassy in Karachi. Right? They'll tell us what's happening. What to do," I huff. "See? I have the phone number on my list."

We are in the centre of Lahore, parked beside a little garden in front of the American Express office. Across the street is a fancy hotel with a "Closed" sign on the front door and all the lights turned out. But wait a minute, I see someone inside. We bang on the door, and a small dark-haired man opens it and steps outside. His name tag shows us that he is the manager of the hotel.

"We are closed. I sent the staff home," he says.

"But we need a place to stay. With a phone. We're Canadian," I plead with alarm, and point to the new Canadian flag sticker on the back bumper of the Beetle.

His kind but worried eyes tell us he understands. He is a good man.

"Yes, our situation here is very serious," he says. "The Indians attacked just outside Lahore this afternoon, near the airport. It's a surprise to everyone. You must leave Lahore as soon as you can. Tomorrow morning. Then you will have nothing to worry about. Our guard can stay here with you tonight. He will try to help if you need him, but he doesn't speak English."

Soon Ross and I are hiding with the guard, a kind-looking man, older than we are, in a dark room on the fifth floor, the best accommodation in the hotel. The lights are off, the curtains are drawn. There is a radio and a phone and they both work. Shortly, three pairs of eyes are peeking, in turn, out into the quiet, dark night. We strain to look and listen. What's happening?

Nothing, it seems. The officials are still running around blackwashing headlights and blowing their whistles. We can't see any other people. Is the gunfire getting closer? Are those real fighter jets overhead?

"Maybe I'm dreaming this is happening to me and everything will be all right tomorrow," I whisper into the silence.

"Oh, it's real," Ross says.

Then a sound I know from the movies and old World War II newsreels wails through the night. Air raid sirens. The men running around on the street are uniformed now. The army. We don't know whose. Jets—Sabres, Ross tells me—are screaming overhead. I don't know what a Sabre is, and none of us knows which air force it is. Maybe both. India and Pakistan. The radio blasts out the news, in Urdu. Finally, we locate the BBC signal. The situation in Pakistan is dark, they say. Right. We know that. It is very dark. Now tell us something new, like how do we get out of here?

Feet. We will abandon the car and walk away like every-one else.

We try and try and try again to reach the Canadian embassy in Karachi by phone. The line is busy. Now it's dead. Where are they? How can they leave us stranded?

Has our Canada abandoned us?

We had a new pride in Canada that year, 1965. After forty years of committee squabbling and Canada's Centennial fast approaching, our government finally got serious and voted on a new flag that was flown for the first time on February 15. Our mothers sent us Canadian flag stickers, Canadian flag baseball caps, and Canadian flag pins. The new flag, with its simple red and white design, sparked conversation everywhere we went and helped us make friends. It symbolized our values—respect, peace, justice, and tolerance—and helped guide us in our travels. Though we don't have a flag sticker on our bumper now, we fly the Canadian flag year-round on our house in Calgary. It still sparks conversation.

But that time, in Lahore, we felt abandoned. We needed to put another cap on, or fly another flag, so to speak.

"Maybe we should exchange our Canadian flag for a red cross and blast through the front line," Ross says wishfully. I can almost see our options trickling through his brain. There aren't many.

We decide to phone the British embassy. First ring, they answer. Good, so far. They say they are evacuating British citizens by the northern route to Afghanistan. That is the route we were on today.

Ross says he knows now that route isn't safe. "Those bridges with the antiaircraft guns are the first things they'll blow up. I'll phone the American embassy."

He is connected right away and then reports. "They say they are evacuating their citizens to Afghanistan on another route to the northwest, by Sargodha. Those guys really know what they're doing."

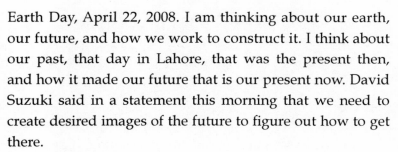

Earth Day, April 22, 2008. I am thinking about our earth, our future, and how we work to construct it. I think about our past, that day in Lahore, that was the present then, and how it made our future that is our present now. David Suzuki said in a statement this morning that we need to create desired images of the future to figure out how to get there.

We did our best.

"We are more scared now than we were then," Ross said last night. "It's a good thing I didn't know what I know now. By the time we figured it all out, we were back at the Afghan border."

September 7, 1965. The early morning is cool and hushed. The fighter jets have stopped fighting; the streets are deserted. We boil some eggs and coffee on the little camp stove we set up in the room, share breakfast with our guard, and say our thank-yous and goodbyes. We are going to fill up the car with gas and leave Lahore, on the American route.

"What do you mean there's no gas?" we gasp in unison.

"The military has locked the tanks. Sorry. There is no gas except for the military," the gas station attendant says.

Ross hands the man a wad of bills. "Please. Give me a little gas. Just a little."

"I am so sorry. Gas is for emergency. The war."

"But I need to go home, this is an emergency," I sob. "My mother wants me home."

"Yes. I know; I understand you have to leave quickly. You must leave Pakistan. I will give you just a little, to get out of Lahore."

But not enough to drive across the desert to the west.

And so we begin our search for gasoline. It is a team performance, with Ross the polite, calm, determined one and me the borderline hysteric, wailing miserably. A new song and dance for us. Half a litre at a time, our gas tank begins to fill. But not enough for the desert. Walking out of Lahore is a distinct possibility.

In time, out of nowhere, a young Pakistani man about our age rides toward us on a scooter, an old Vespa, just like the one we had in London. "Do you need help?" he asks.

"We are looking for gasoline. Petrol. So we can get out of here." We explain we were driving to India from London, but now we need to go back to Afghanistan until it's safer here.

"But the gasoline stations have all been locked by the military," the young man says. "Let me think. Yes. I know where I can find you a jerry can. And my friend can fill it up for you. That way, at least, you will have enough to get you away from the city. It's not safe here. Come to my house. We'll get you organized. My mother is sick, so none of us want to leave until tomorrow. Would you like to have lunch with us? My sisters and I speak English, and my mother is an English teacher. They would love to meet you."

John Herbert and his three sisters laugh and chatter constantly as they move around their modern bungalow and garden, keeping us amused, cooking our lunch, and tending to their bedridden mother, who says she is feeling much better now. Our spirits perk up with conversation about homes and siblings, and our lunch of hot home-cooked chicken curry.

With a new jerry can full of gas, for which no one would take any money, we say goodbye, promising to write when we are safely back in Afghanistan.

(We've not forgotten the Herbert family, though we lost track of them some time ago. For years, we sent letters back and forth, and John came to visit us once in Montreal when he was doing his graduate studies in the States. We live with their model of hospitality and their lessons of warmth, kindness, and helping strangers.)

Thousands are leaving the city. Most are walking; others are on carts pulled by oxen or in chariots drawn by donkeys. We slowly chug along in the Beetle.

The dusty road bends around banana groves, farms, and a few settlements. Eventually, the traffic thins — we have come too far for the walkers, the bullocks, and the donkeys.

Suddenly, late in the afternoon, we are stopped by a long line of cars blocking the road. It's the Americans, and they tell us they're waiting for gasoline before they can move on. We share their anxiety, but I am focused on self preservation and am sorry I can't share our full tank and jerry can, before we pass hundreds of cars and several armoured vehicles in camouflage.

We're proud of our teamwork. We have gas, we have a tent, and we have food. We'll be okay.

Before it gets too late, we want to stop somewhere in the countryside, as far as we can from the fighting. Our tourist pamphlets show that we're close to a government rest house — not quite a DAK bungalow, where the British high officials stay, but a small house good enough for lower bureaucrats and travellers.

There it is. In the middle of the farmland stands a small British-style bungalow with neat rows of trees around it.

The sun is setting, and a group of five or six men is sitting on the porch talking. We get out of the car and walk over. One large man, wearing traditional Pakistani Shalwar Kameez and a Jinnah cap, sits back in his chair, strangely pumping one bare foot back and forth, back and forth. What is he doing? He looks as though he is in some weird kind of trance. Straightening his leg, bending it, straightening, and bending. As we walk toward the porch entrance, I see a dirty thin rope tied to his right big toe. The other end is attached to something. There. Look up. Way up. The rope attached to the man's toe is also attached to an enormous Persian-Baluch rug hung from the ceiling. Strong geometric patterns in shiny hues of navy blue, rust, and aubergine swing back and pause. Swing forward and pause. Repeat. This is our air-conditioning system. This will be a good place to stay.

We are the only guests. Our beds are made with clean, white linens; the pillows are just right—big and soft. Someone prepares us a simple supper.

I feel safe in this place. I can sleep now.

But the night is long, very long. There is so much noise. This is supposed to be quiet countryside. People are talking and moaning, dogs are growling and fighting, donkeys are braying, cocks crowing. There are fires in the fields. We aren't worried about being blown up, but we know something is not right.

The morning is still; the sky is an uncanny, beautiful clear blue. We are on the road again, and there are open fields all around, lush and green. We don't see anyone travelling except a man riding a bicycle. He is holding a large piece of a banana tree over his head.

"That's his camouflage," Ross says, laughing.

A moment later, two jets appear out of nowhere and begin a fierce dogfight directly above us. We stare in awe. Then as quickly as they appeared, they fly away and disappear.

"Was that real?" Neither of us knows.

We found out later that day in Peshawar that "the American route" took us directly by the Pakistani air force base Sargodha. All these years, I have been wondering if what we saw was a dream, so last night I Googled "Sargodha. September 1965." I learned that Sargodha was considered to be part of the front line during Pakistan's three-week war with India. The Indian air force executed six swift attacks on Sargodha the day we drove by.

"It's real," Ross said, looking over my shoulder at the computer screen. "It's a good thing I didn't know it then."

I didn't sleep last night either, thinking about what is real and not real.

The drive is long, tiresome, and sweltering, through flat scrub and desert. About 6:00 p.m. we arrive in Peshawar for the second time this week, and it is a different city now. The tension is palpable. It is packed with foreigners trying to get out of the country through the Afghan border, and the hotels are full. We camp in the garden of a DAK bungalow while air raid sirens terrorize us through the night.

Our priority now is to get our documents in order to reenter Afghanistan, and we are surprised how simple the process is for us. Soon we're on our way, back to Kabul through the Khyber Pass. This time it is daylight, and we are on the right side of the road. That is, the left.

The Khyber Pass is swarming with tension. Tribal people guarding the bridges have long rifles and bandoliers laden with fat cartridges swung over their shoulders and across their chests. Strapped around their waists are thick leather sheaths with long swords and knives. We smile, wave, point to our Canadian flag, and carry on. We don't feel any fear now that we are going home to Kabul.

The Red Cross workers are waiting for us at the border. They say we are the first refugees to arrive and ply us with sandwiches and tea before we drive on to Kabul and our campsite on the Khyber Dam.

our campsite in bamiyan

salaam aleikum: peace to you
(AfGHANISTAN)

*T*HE AFGHANISTAN WE KNEW then was beautiful, exciting to explore, and full of hope for a healthy future. It was a good place to live in 1965, while Pakistan and India got themselves sorted out so we could continue our journey eastward on the Silk Road. We were alive. We were safe. We had jobs. We were settling into the new reality that our adventure had been temporarily thwarted by a war.

My sister Jeanne, who was five years old at the time, remembers the agony of our families in Quebec. They phoned each other back and forth, and they kept in touch with Canadian government officials. "Tell them to come home," the advisor said. Dad, the one who never disciplined and the most diplomatic of our four parents, was judged to be the one who would probably have the most impact on us. He was assigned the task of replying to the telegram we had sent, telling them we were safe in Kabul. "Advise your return to Europe at once. Will send money. Dad," it read.

Mom and Dad are worried, and I'm scared and homesick. But my heart tells me to stay here awhile. I don't know why. Yet.

Everything I see around me is brown. Gravel streets are lined with murky ditches, and adobe houses hide behind mud walls. Children are covered in dirt, pus seeping from their kohl-infected eyes, noses streaming with thick mucus.

Brown—a colour that is inconsistently dark. I even feel brown with worries and fears rolling around inside my head.

We live in a new suburb of Kabul, near the university. We moved here from our campsite on the Khyber Dam when our new friends in the American Peace Corps suggested it was going to be a cold winter and they had extra space in their house. In spite of the gloom I feel, our street is filled with cheerful activity, and slowly it is drawing me into a new life. There are people everywhere. Gangs of children run between packs of dogs; goats and chickens graze through the garbage. Older youths walk by on their way to the campus. Most of the young women carrying armloads of heavy textbooks are dressed like I am, in modest skirts and short-sleeve blouses. Other women are covered, their mysterious blue and mauve burkas silently swirling around as they stroll to the local market with friends. Men wear long shirts and baggy trousers, and some wear turbans. They walk hand in hand, drive in little vans or donkey carts, and ride bicycles. Everyone is carrying something, doing things, going somewhere. Afghanistan is a busy place.

Protected from the chaos and excitement of the street by a wall, our house has a small courtyard inside with stairs at one end leading to a flat roof. I love the roof. From here, I immerse myself in the lives of our Afghan neighbours. I look down into their courtyard and watch meals being prepared, children being disciplined, and grandparents being cared for. This morning a threadbare carpet in the centre of the yard was rolled up and replaced with a massive traditional red and black Afghan carpet. In a hive of activity, a feast is spread out, and from my perch I watch an uncharacteristically sombre group of people gather.

It is a funeral. My neighbours are honouring the life of a grandparent who passed away earlier today.

As it does on most frosty October mornings, the sun shines and the sky is the colour of lapis lazuli. Children, little bundles of rags vying for attention, surround me trying to teach me their language, and I do my best to teach them mine. They mimic me in a rapid jumble of words without meaning. "Hello. My name is Nancy. What's your name?"

Minding the younger children are two older girls, about ten. The tiny face veils sewed into their new blue burkas constantly slip out of place. Undaunted by being blinded, tripping and falling, the girls deftly yank the fronts of their burkas over their heads, to their shoulders, so they can see and continue playing. Batman style. I am in awe of their bright, confident demeanours and resourcefulness.

The Americans and Russians are competing for favour in Afghanistan. Foreign aid is big business. Schools are

119

better today than they were a few years ago, there are more good health clinics, and food is plentiful. I don't dare ask about clean drinking water, sanitation, and toilets. It's an embarrassing subject that's quickly avoided in most cultures.

The new Russian bread factory is the pride of Kabul, and even the Americans love it. The factory is the city's bread of life — not only does it make food, it also makes jobs for women and men. Hundreds of Afghan factory workers dressed in crisp white lab coats fill it each day.

Though they love the fresh European-style bread, our American friends are not as impressed with the Russians as we are. "Russian spies are everywhere. Communists," they tell us.

"Don't worry about us. We'll be careful," I reply.

"We'll see the Russians for ourselves, get to know them," Ross says. "We'll visit the Russian Embassy and take a tour. Learn something. Maybe we'll find out how to get to Samarkand."

The Russian Embassy is an immense new white fortress in stark brown landscape. A huge white iron fence surrounds it. An electrified fence. The gate is closed. Russian soldiers carrying machine guns are on guard.

"Well. I've seen soldiers with guns before. No worries. We're Canadian. Everybody loves us," I boast with confident superiority as we drive toward the gate and honk. Yes, of course it opens. Slowly. Six inches.

"STOP."

Three armed soldiers charge out of the gatehouse, bound over, and bang our window, ready to shoot. We point wildly to the new Canadian flag on the windshield. "Us? We're Canadian."

"Halt! Halt! Get out of here. Go away."

Humbled, we steal away. In the rearview mirror, we see the guards still watching us with baffled looks. Did our Canadian bravado leave a good impression?

(I'm still wondering.)

We take a break from Kabul for a few days and drive up into the Hindu Kush mountains toward Bamiyan. Once a thriving centre for Buddhist art and culture, it is famous for its 1,500-year-old standing Buddhas, the largest in the world. While we're in the area we'll visit Band-e-Amir, a group of deep azure lakes hidden at 3,000 metres of elevation in the desolate central range.

Driving north from Kabul on the sleek new Russian-built highway through the Salang Pass, we turn west after a couple hours. New asphalt morphs into wretched track. The flat tire is inevitable. We congratulate ourselves that this is only the first flat tire and drive to the side of the road into a pretty field to change it.

Two small girls in brightly coloured rag dresses come to watch, crouching down on their haunches. Their eyes shine with curiosity, and smiling politely, they clasp their little hands to their chests and bow their heads, as if in prayer. "*Salaam aleikum*," peace to you, they say. "*Salaam aleikum*," I reply, and our friendship begins. Eventually, their parents come over to us and stand ready to help. *Milmastia*, hospitality, I am learning, is the sacred duty of tribesmen toward guests in their rugged and unforgiving terrain. I am a captive of their quiet, unassuming friendliness.

With the tire replaced and our hearts warmed, we drive on through the mountains and eventually a lush green valley, framed by snowcapped Hindu Kush mountains, comes into view. By the river, a gravel road, neatly lined with poplar trees, directs us through orchards, laden with nuts and fruit, to a cluster of family compounds. This is Bamiyan. We set up camp on a hill overlooking giant sandstone Buddhas and ancient monasteries. A group of elegant men, dressed in long, multicoloured wool cloaks and furry karakul caps, comes over to say hello and asks us to join them for tea at their table nearby. Together we watch the sun set, casting its warm glow on the marvels of history we're all here to see.

On our trip back to Kabul the new road is jammed. Trucks grind along ahead of us, brightly painted with scenes of the magnificent mountains, fields, and lakes we visited. Piled on top are sacks of grain and dozens of tribesmen embraced by bandoliers, bullets, and massive rifles. They are celebrating the Jeshin holy day. Laughing and waving, they aim their rifles at us. They're playing, urging us to join them in the fun. We laugh, somewhat tentatively, I admit, and return their waves. It does not occur to me to be afraid. We are all celebrating the holiday.

Before we go back to our house, we stop at Kabul market, with merchants selling, shoppers buying, and onlookers craving as they crowd into the little shops. Today we need to pay for a present we bought for ourselves last week. We missed a digit in the confusing math that transformed our Canadian dollars to afghanis. The carpet would cost ten times more than we calculated.

"Take it," the shopkeeper had said, "bring me the money when you can."

This time we hand him a great wad of afghanis, and he stashes it in his pocket without counting.

"*Tashekur*. Thank you. I trusted you to come back," he says.

We shake hands and move on. Later, we are surprised to meet our carpet shopkeeper in another store. He takes the wad of afghanis we gave him from his pocket and buys a transistor radio. I understand at this moment that the world is becoming more accessible, and the Afghanistan we know will change.

December 2002. Snow is falling softly outside my window, and a thick cloud settles on Grotto Mountain. I want to remember Afghanistan the way it was, full of hope. The haunting image in today's paper is a ghostlike figure, a woman wandering through a Kabul I do not know — homes in rubble, streets dominated by violence — a joyless place.

"Families Find Homes Wherever They Can," reads the headline.

The fields are laced with land mines; there are no fruit and nut trees. The rivers are mere trickles.

The giant Buddhas were blown up.

Then the terrorists attacked again, in New York and Washington.

Now Canada is at war in Afghanistan.

I don't know why my mother kept the stacks of letters I sent. Did she know I would need them someday, to help me remember how it was?

I can't throw out our old Afghan carpet that's worn to shreds. Repeated elements in it connect with one another, although each element has its own special characteristic. It reminds me of people. Although we're all different, we have common qualities that connect us.

A while ago I heard someone on the television speaking to Canadian armed forces in Afghanistan. She was crying and said that in her soul, in her bones, the sacrifices Canadian soldiers endure would make way for peace.

Sometimes I cry too. In our living room there is a large black and white photograph of the little girls who watched us change the flat tire. They should be grown women now, and I would like to talk with them. I would ask them if they're still making friends and saying, "Peace to you." Their curious eyes and lively smiles in the photograph keep me hoping that someday our story about Afghanistan will have a happier ending.

the giant buddhas, the beetle, and me

nomads crossing boundaries

XIII

do we take the road to samarkand?

And softly through the silence beat the bells
Along the Golden Road to Samarkand.
We travel not for trafficking alone;
By hotter winds our fiery hearts are fanned:
For lust of knowing what should not be known
We take the Golden Road to Samarkand.

FROM "THE GOLDEN ROAD TO SAMARKAND"
BY JAMES ELROY FLECKER, 1900

OCTOBER 1965. It is getting cold, and when I look out my window I see snow blanketing the high rocky peaks of the Hindu Kush. Friends here tell me winters are severe. They say it will lock you in until spring. Even without snow I feel trapped in Afghanistan. We can't get out through the Khyber Pass because of the India-Pakistan war. The other

127

border crossings into Pakistan and Iran are shut because of
the cholera epidemic. The border with Russia is uncertain
because of the Cold War.

I want to go home. Right now.

"We should be able to leave soon, before the winter,"
Ross says. "I heard a rumour that the northern border's
going to open soon." He looks at a map — weather, war,
cholera, and politics won't stop him from pursuing his
dream of travelling to exotic places. He points to the vast,
murky green area north of Afghanistan, which we know as
Russia, the Soviet Union. There we note the Soviet Socialist
Republics of Turkmenistan, Tajikistan, and Uzbekistan,
which I have never heard of before. "The boundary up there
is 1,900 kilometres long," Ross says. "Once we find a way to
get into the Soviet Union, there will be a way to get back to
Europe. Samarkand is a huge city, and it's just ninety-seven
kilometres from the Afghan border."

My discomfort and crankiness about the prospect of
going through Russia grow. I don't feel myself these days,
and I cry a lot. I miss my family, and I write them almost
every day. A letter from one of them every month or so only
makes me feel worse.

"We don't know anyone who's been there." My
voice begins to break as I muster my argument. "To get
to Samarkand, we have to find a way to get across that
border into Russia. We need papers. Maps. Information.
Remember? Last week the Russian Embassy slammed their
gate in our faces. They think we're Americans."

Ross doesn't give up and says quietly, "The roads won't

128

be much of a problem. They're good." His calm voice doesn't make me feel better. We both know that Russia and the United States compete with each other to build the roads in Afghanistan, and tensions are high. The Soviets built the highway from Kandahar north to the border, and last year they opened the new highway from Kabul, north through the Salang Pass. The year before that, the Americans opened the highway in the south from Kabul to Kandahar. They are all protecting what they think is their turf.

"As a matter of fact," I protest, "I feel like I'm in the middle of another James Bond movie here, with everyone spying on one another, flexing their muscles, and doling out propaganda. They even boast about their nuclear arms." Rumours of a third world war are not uncommon around Kabul. We are used to tall tales, but the Cuban missile crisis two years ago and the Berlin crisis the year before that haven't exactly made me feel safer.

Our new American Peace Corps friends in Kabul think we're crazy for even thinking about going to Samarkand and the land of antifreedom, antireligion. "Why would anyone want to go there?" they ask.

"Why? Samarkand was one of the most important cities on earth. It was the crown jewel of the Silk Road. Everyone went to Samarkand — Genghis Khan, Alexander, Timur, Marco Polo — they were all there. It was the centre of civilization." Ross studied Samarkand's famous mosques and palaces in his school of architecture at McGill, and to prove his points, he hauls out a textbook he's brought on our trip, his bible for travel, Sir Banister Fletcher's *A History*

129

of Architecture, first published in 1896. "You can see for yourself in this book. Samarkand is so close. We'll never be able to get there again."

I can't beat Ross's enthusiasm, and he has almost persuaded me to go back to Canada via the Soviet Union. Our American friends are aghast.

I look at the drawings in Fletcher's book that are the substance of "the golden road that leads to Samarkand" in the blurry fairy tales and poems I've read. It is a city of domes and minarets that teems with beauty and people in flowing robes.

Yesterday we learned that the northwestern border with Iran would open in a few days. They will let some people into Iran if they have papers proving they've been inoculated against cholera within the past two weeks. The immunization clinic has a foul reputation, and we still don't know how to get into Russia. Everything is risky and there are choices to make. Cholera or hepatitis.

I opt for hepatitis and find my way to a dirty, unlit "health" clinic. There is no choice really. The syringe is grungy; the needle is long with barbs. I grit through the ordeal, then leave with the "health" papers that go with the needle to get out of Afghanistan.

We study the map again and realize that the big red highway deteriorates into a thin, white dysfunctional track and disappears altogether at the Afghan-Soviet Union border. Although my "lust of knowing" the road to Samarkand is improving, I feel somewhat self-satisfied when I realize that we will not be able to get there from Afghanistan.

"Don't worry. We'll try to get into Russia from that spot," Ross says, pointing to another big red road, this one leading toward Samarkand from northeastern Iran.

Ross still doesn't give up easily.

We head west out of Kabul to Kandahar, then travel north to Herat, where we will go west again and cross the border into Iran. At every intersection there are roadblocks and military police who wave their machine guns around to stop us. We have to show them our "health" papers. From large green garbage bags, the soldiers dole out pills with "tetracycline" printed on them. We must swallow the pills in front of them before the army will let us go on. I recoil.

Before we left Kabul, I checked tetracycline in the nursing textbook I brought with me. "Look, Ross. It says, 'Women of childbearing age must not take tetracycline. It could harm a foetus.' Oh god. It's the principle of it. Forcing me to swallow those pills. Who knows? I could be pregnant."

I bravely dip my hand into the big green bag and haul out a handful of pills. My brain races into high gear. The military and their nasty guns won't defeat me. I am a chipmunk now and hide the pills in my cheeks while, for the benefit of the military, I pretend to swallow them. I gag and spit them out when we're out of their sight.

The system works perfectly.

But the plan to go to Samarkand doesn't. The borders from Iran across the Iron Curtain are closed because of the cholera epidemic, and our Silk Road journey is on hold.

January 2005. A book three inches thick, with discoloured, dog-eared pages and half of a faded blue cardboard cover, is on our living room bookshelf in Calgary. Just as forty years earlier, we're using our Fletcher's *History of Architecture* to make plans for continuing our journey along the Silk Road and fill in some of the gaps we missed so long ago. For forty years we've been telling stories about our 1965 trip, but until now we've only been able to dream about going to those elusive, obscure places, like Samarkand, that we didn't get to.

"I'll go to celebrate getting my old-age pension," Ross laughs.

"I don't suppose we'll be able to get travel medical insurance," I reply tersely.

"True. We'll have to self-insure. If we don't go this year, we may never get there."

As usual in our discussions, my enthusiasm grows as we talk through our fantasies for travel. I immerse myself in reading more about the Silk Road, and the words of the poet Flecker speak to me again: "for the lust of knowing what should not be known." This time I will "take the Golden Road to Samarkand."

A friend suggests we e-mail his contact in Kyrgyzstan, Ishen, who is from a traditional shepherding family. In the early 1990s, when Kyrgyzstan was undergoing drastic social and economic change transitioning to an independent republic after the collapse of the Soviet Union, Ishen lost his job as a teacher. A Swiss development agency helped his family start up a horse-trekking business. He e-mails us back saying that he will arrange to take us on horses into the high meadows of the Tian Shan Mountains north of Afghanistan, and he puts us in touch with a community-based tourism company in Kyrgyzstan and a guide-interpreter in Uzbekistan to help us facilitate the rest of the trip. Together with all of them and our good friends Lynne and Bill, who have been listening to our stories for years and want to come this time, we work out the details.

The plan is this: We will fly to Bishkek from London and, after a day's rest, fly on to spend another day in Tashkent, Uzbekistan's ancient but cosmopolitan capital. With a jet lag of three days' travel behind us, we will be ready to go on to Khiva, one of the country's many historic walled Silk Road cities that Marco Polo visited. The city is a museum in itself, packed with turquoise-tiled domes of mosques, palaces, tombs, and ancient madrassas, Islamic schools, and cloistered courtyards. I've seen soft pastel pictures of these ancient cities in fairy-tale storybooks I read my grandchildren, and Ross backs up my images with photographs in his architecture books.

From Khiva we will drive through depleted cotton fields, from the Russian era of vast monoculture, to Bukhara, Central Asia's ancient cultural heart and one place traders along the Silk Road, including Marco, never missed. Today there remain dozens of important historical monuments and ancient bazaars.

"The town is magnificent, but this is one place you really should go shopping and look for a good rug to take home," our neighbour who belongs to the "New Calgary Rug and

Textile Club" tells us.

I'm keen. That old carpet we bought in Afghanistan has fallen apart, and I want to replace it. Though I can't replace our experience buying a rug in Kabul, who knows what shopping for a rug in Bukhara will bring?

Then we will travel on to Samarkand, a key Silk Road city whose name, even today, evokes visions of the romantic and exotic in stories told by poets and playwrights of another era. It is the ancient capital of Timur the Lame — Tamerlane — who in the fourteenth century rampaged through Iran, Iraq, Syria, and eastern Turkey, stole the riches, and kidnapped the artisans to build the palaces, mosques, and tombs of Samarkand.

"You will love it. My uncle has a carpet factory in Samarkand," Parwen, a young Afghan refugee friend I know, tells me. "Here's the name of their place. They will welcome you."

What are my chances of finding them in Samarkand? I ask myself. Even if I can't find them, looking for them will be an adventure.

From Samarkand, we will drive straight across the volatile and dangerous Fergana Valley just north of Afghanistan to Andijan. We will stay one night before transferring across the Kyrgyz border and changing vans, drivers, and guide-interpreters.

The drive along southern Kyrgyzstan into China will be via the Irkeshtam Pass, which is, according to our guidebook, "the latest border post to open along an ancient branch of the Silk Road. Spectacular views of the Pamirs."

"Great. New pass. New roads. No worries there," we tell each other. We will not be far from Afghanistan, but unlike our trip of forty years ago, we will be on the other side of that border that is still closed to us. But not to danger and the heroin smugglers.

Afghanistan, so rich in my memories, is even closer to me now as I plan our trip. I am preoccupied by a fugue of thought. Could, or better still should, I have predicted years ago when we were so far away that Canada would play a major role in Afghanistan today, trying to stamp out terrorism and put peace back together? Were there signs? How could we have avoided the mess we're in?

Once we have reached the relative safety of northwestern China we'll visit the renowned centre of Silk Road travel, Kashgar, and put down a foot on the Taklamakan Desert near Mongolia. The drive back to Kyrgyzstan will be over the rough and difficult Torugart Pass. We'll pick up another Kyrgyz guide and a van and drive through the mountains, camping in yurts, to Barskoon village on Lake Issyk Kul. I dream of floating in it, the world's second-largest saltwater lake, surrounded by the majestic Tian Shans. It is here that we will meet Ishen and his family and begin our horse trek.

From the comfort of my sunny office at home in Calgary, I e-mail back and forth every day for weeks planning our trip with our contacts in Central Asia. Nothing is impossible. I feel I know them all well now, and they are my friends. I know their families, and they know mine. I stash hard copies of precious communications in a file to take with us.

Well ahead of our planned July departure, all is in place

except our visas. Wow. This is easy travelling, I think.

BBC News release, March 2005. "Protests in Kyrgyzstan escalate following a second round of parliamentary elections." Protesters take over official buildings in the south and in Bishkek, the capital. Some say it's a revolution. Rallies call for the president's resignation. He flees to Russia, and the Supreme Court annuls the result of the election. An important member of parliament is shot dead.

"Don't worry," our Kyrgyz contacts say. "The situation is serious now, but it will be okay soon. There will be another election just before you get here in July. That should settle things down. But of course it is your choice to come or not."

My friend the Internet keeps me apprised almost hourly of what's going on along our planned route. I think back to our ignorance of the situation in Russia forty years ago when rumours were the only information we had. Now all the information is readily available, but a major problem still exists. The computer can't tell me whether it's safe for us to go to Samarkand. Lynne, Bill, Ross, and I discuss our options. I lose sleep thinking that my dream of filling the gap in my travel along the Silk Road will vanish and our plans will fail. Again.

Then our problems get worse.

BBC News, May 13, 2005. "The city of Andijan in eastern Uzbekistan is gripped by unrest. Gunmen storm the prison and release inmates, some of whom have been accused of Islamic militancy. Troops open fire on protesters. The government puts the overall death toll at 180."

June 8, 2005. *The New York Times* reports that Human

Rights Watch labels the unrest in Uzbekistan "a massacre," saying hundreds of civilians were gunned down. Wounded people who survived the night of May 13 were shot down the next day by troops moving through the bodies. Some claim the death toll is 745. There are fears about the safety of Westerners in the country. The United States suspends its presence at the Uzbek air base near the Afghan border and withdraws its citizens.

I hit the Canadian government travel reports site in a panic. "U. Uzbekistan. Official Travel Warning." In red. "Avoid all travel." Knowing this site well from other experiences, I search for some sign of hope in the situation. I find it a few paragraphs later. "The decision to travel is the sole responsibility of the traveller. Travellers are responsible for their own safety. Canadians should contact the official Consulate of Canada in Tashkent for further information." So. They should let us in. I phone the Canadian foreign affairs officer at the Uzbek desk in Ottawa. Then I phone the Canadian consulate in Tashkent. "I'm getting older," I tell them, "and I don't have a lot of time left to complete my Silk Road travel." I explain I want to discuss the impact of the revolution on tourism and tell them about our online relationship with our guides and their families in Central Asia. "They will suffer if their tourist business declines. How will they manage? They don't have a safety net like we do here in Canada."

We are thousands of miles apart, but we all agree. Ordinary people in Central Asia will pay a terrible price.

"If you decide to go ahead with your plan, be very, very

cautious. Call us if we can help," they suggest.

Lynne, Bill, Ross, and I meet again. None of us have discussed our trip with our children, and we hope they haven't listened to the news. We don't want to worry them any sooner than necessary. We agree to vote on whether to go. We are a team. It will be all of us or none.

My stomach riots with anxiety and a pull between what is right and wrong. "Wouldn't it be wrong not to go now? They are depending on us. On our dollars. Even more important is the fact that, by sticking with the plans we've made with them, we can help bolster their morale and their confidence."

"We should go to see for ourselves what's going on. It will be our last chance," Ross says.

"There will be stories. Things to learn," Lynne says.

Our meeting is not long. We will leave July 14.

Now we just have to get the visas.

Time is short for getting them. The visa into China is easy. We can get it ourselves in Calgary. Overnight. The visa for Kyrgyzstan shouldn't be a problem either. We can get it when we arrive at the airport in Bishkek.

Getting visas into Uzbekistan is a different story. There is no Uzbek embassy or consulate in Canada. We need to send our passports to New York. I e-mail the consulate there for more information. No reply. I phone. No answer.

We've heard there are special companies that will do all the work for us to get the Uzbek visa. They can get us through all the necessary hoops and, for a hefty price, obtain the required travel documents and permits.

I try phoning New York again. A sterile monotone recording says, "This is the Consulate of Uzbekistan in New York. We do not answer telephone calls. Please refer to our website." I refer to the website. Again. There is no information for Canadians. I phone our contact in Tashkent in despair.

"Don't worry," he tells me. "E-mail us a copy of your passport, and we'll send it to New York with a letter of recommendation. We'll send you a reference number."

We are not keen to send our precious Canadian passport information to, what seems to us, a nonexistent Uzbek consulate in New York for who knows how long.

So finally we decide to simply pay the big dollars and ask a visa procurement company here in Calgary to do the work for us.

"Yes, we can get visas for any country within a few days. Uzbekistan? Uzbekistan, you say? Uh-oh. Well. I am so sorry. Uzbekistan is the ONLY country we don't get visas for."

"Why?"

"It's been horrible. Impossible. We tried last year for a woman who was going on a trek. It was a mess. We just couldn't get the visa. She ended up not going."

"But our travel company in Uzbekistan has already sent our information to New York. All we have to do is fill out the forms and get someone like your company to take our passports into the consulate in New York and pick them up when it's done."

"Sorry."

I search the Internet. The Uzbek embassy in Washington lists a visa service.

"Uzbekistan. No problem. Sure, we can do that," says a pleasant, enthusiastic-sounding man with a Boston accent when I call.

I breathe a sigh of thankfulness.

"Oh. You're Canadians? Really? Uh-oh. I'm sorry. We are unable get visas for Canadians. It's against international law."

I groan, and he feels my worry.

"I'm very sorry. I want to help. Here's the name of a company in Calgary that you can get in touch with."

"But I've already contacted them. They say they can't do it. It's too difficult for them."

"Look," he says, "it's not all that hard. It's Uzbekistan. You have to understand what they want, and you do exactly as you're told. Make absolutely certain you make no mistakes filling out the forms. I'll help you by phone. Then you can send the documents to New York by return courier. You won't have a problem."

So we download all the forms, and the four of us go through each set of papers meticulously to ensure every word is spelled correctly, the right number of passport photos are attached, the correct number of U.S. dollars is included in a registered American bank draft, and our precious passports are in the envelope. We request expedited service. We send the package on Monday by return FedEx (ONLY FEDEX, the instructions say) and expect never to see our passports again.

It is Wednesday and a package arrives. In it are our passports, with the Uzbek visas stamped in them.

"Yay! Let's have another meeting. To celebrate. We're really going this time. It's looking good."

July 14, 2005. I am daydreaming in a remote back corner of Calgary Airport with my travel mates, waiting for our flight to London and then on to Bishkek. Is this hushed, insipid beginning to our holiday a sign, perhaps a foreshadowing of an ordinary, rather than the exotic, holiday I expect? Perhaps it is a calm before a storm, a breather before we delve into cultures we do not know or understand.

Today is the day that celebrates the storming of the Bastille by French peasants and the beginning of the French Revolution. I remember the Bastille Day parties at my grandparents' house in Toronto, with my grandfather smoking his cigars and all the ladies dressed in silk, pinching long silver cigarette holders between their lips. I drift off. There is a buzz of flamboyant, animated discussion. I can't understand what they're saying, but I am awestruck by their speaking French, waving their arms about and exuding intrigue. Knowing what my grandfather valued, I like to think that they were celebrating freedom and talking about democracy.

Only four days ago, the very first democratic elections were held in Kyrgyzstan. Ishen and his family and our contacts with NoviNomad, the community-based tourist association, are ecstatic. They say they have a future they can look forward to now.

Bishkek, Uzbekistan, July 17, 2005, 5:00 a.m. Everything around me is grey, early morning grey, terminal-building grey, uniformed-soldiers grey. Big fat planes, grey with U.S. flags painted on them, are all around our little plane on the tarmac. Ross says they are bombers. Never having seen a bomber, I wouldn't have known. But now I'm scared. And hot. And sweaty. There are long lines to go through. The security line, the passport line, the visa line, the cashier line, and the security line. Again. Then we drag ourselves through the baggage line, the customs line, and finally out of the secured area into the public concourse, where the touts are waiting to prey on the pure and the innocent. That's us.

But wait a minute. There she is, waving and smiling. I didn't recognize her from my Internet conversations, but I know it is Zamira, our guide-interpreter. What a bright, happy picture of health she is. Her dark Mongolian eyes, high cheekbones, rosy skin, and long, shiny black hair strongly characterize her Kyrgyz ethnicity. A delicate, trim figure, she sprints over, hugs, and greets us all. In flawless English she says, "Welcome to our country. We have been waiting for you a long time, and now you are finally here."

I'm okay now. We will take the road to Samarkand this time.

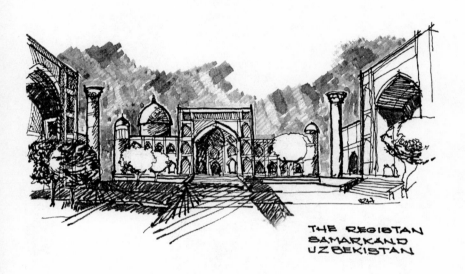

THE REGISTAN
SAMARKAND
UZBEKISTAN

KALTA MINOR
MINARET
KHIVA
UZBEKISTAN

144

SHER DOR
MADRESSA
SAMARKAND
UZBEKISTAN

145

ID KAHN
MOSQUE
KASHGAR
CHINA

146

ID KAHN
MOSQUE
KASHGAR
CHINA

YURT.
BARSKOÖN
VILLAGE
KRYGYZSTAN

LON XING
TEMPLE
SHIJIAZHUANG
CHINA

YÁNGSHOÙ
RIVER LI
CHINA

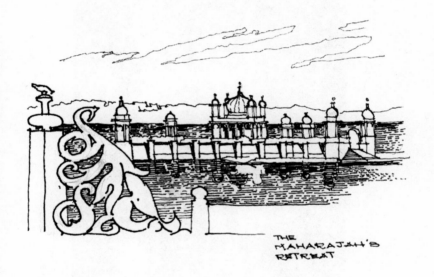

THE
MAHARAJAH'S
RETREAT

151

bukhara

XIV

back to central asia
(KYRGYZSTAN, UZBEKISTAN)

*J*ULY 2005. I feel the moment, the quiet of dawn broken by gentle birdsong. Everyone else here in our little guesthouse in Bishkek is asleep. It feels good to be rested and alone for a while to think about this place and write about it.

After we arrived yesterday, Lynne, Bill, Ross, and I had tea on the patio with Zamira. She told us that, historically, Bishkek was a small Silk Road settlement, one of several along the caravan routes in the Tian Shan Mountains. In 1862 the Russians captured Kyrgyzstan and set up a garrison at Bishkek before they lured Russian peasants to come and farm in the surrounding fertile valleys. When the Soviet Union collapsed, in 1991, Kyrgyzstan declared independence like other Soviet Republics in Central Asia.

In a clear, proud voice, Zamira explains there are forty-six tribes in Kyrgyzstan; only 15 percent of the population is Russian. "We all get along," she says. "When the revolution happened two months ago, in May this year, 5,000 people stormed our 'White House,' our presidential palace in Bishkek. They demanded a free election. But the president ran away, to Russia, to his family." Zamira continues with a huff of disgust. "People are mad he didn't stay to work things out. What was he thinking? That he had done his bit? That scoundrel. That villain."

The diminutive Zamira articulates her thoughts with fierce fluency and conviction. She has benefited from a gift of the Soviet era, education for all, boys and girls, men and women. Her nation's literacy rate is 97 percent.

My thoughts turn to Afghanistan. It's hard for me to believe it's so close, a few kilometres away, but the Afghanistan we knew in 1965 is far away.

I am afraid of Afghanistan now. The literacy rate for women there is 21 percent. Women's lives are marginalized by horrifying discrimination and exclusion from a life I take for granted.

Zamira finished her university degree in tourism management three years ago.

She says, "In our NoviNomad tourism development company, we emphasize development. Our mission is to work with independent drivers, guesthouses, and craft makers. So we skip the middlemen and focus on fair employment practises, or self-employment." The result is that tourists like us experience the real Kyrgyzstan, the people and their homes. "After all, it is people who make a place," Zamira adds.

"Isn't it wonderful that we are all sitting here and talking together about our families, our lives, and politics?" Lynne says. "Forty years ago, we were in the middle of the Cold War. Our countries were enemies then, Zamira. You weren't even born, but you were the enemy," she chuckles softly as our little group sits together on the sunny patio.

It is a dry, hot Sunday morning, and the streets are almost deserted as we walk through the downtown capital area. Wide roads are flanked by Soviet-style, modern, five-story walk-up buildings. I see nothing Asian. To try to fit into the Asia I imagined, I have donned what I thought would be a culturally appropriate outfit for the day: an ankle-length black skirt, a long-sleeve, drip-dry brown shirt, and a head scarf. That's me. Sweat. Sweating. Sweatier. All the others on the street, including other sixty-five-year-old women, are dressed in form-fitting blue jeans and tight cotton T-shirts. I have a lot to learn.

Calgary, March 2009. Is it auspicious that last night, when I got home from a writers group meeting, I found our old *History of Architecture* lying in a pile in the basement, where we are sleeping during renovations? I thumbed through the index like a madwoman. Why is Samarkand not there? Where is Bukhara? I clearly remember the ancient mosques and palaces in it, but they are generic architectural drawings, and Samarkand is not mentioned. There are pages written about Saracenic architecture, Islamic architecture, but the only photographs are of the grand, well-travelled cities of Agra, Cairo, Constantinople, and Jerusalem.

"I am writing a memoir," my colleague had told me one time, "but, you know, really, it's fiction."

"You call your memoir fiction?" I asked him. "I'm struggling to tell what I remember with integrity. My memory is full of stories I've told over and over. Modified through the years, mind you. Can it be possible that my memoir is part fiction too?"

I am distressed that I remember the old pictures of Samarkand we looked at in 1965. Where are they? Why did Fletcher not put them in the book he published in 1896? Was it because in those days, the British were fully occupied in India and China? Or that Samarkand was too remote, in a dangerous desert? That he wrote just what he knew, what he too remembered? These are questions I need to leave for another story. Maybe someday I'll find the pictures of Samarkand we looked at so long ago.

We said goodbye to Zamira yesterday. I was sad to leave so soon, but we'll meet up with her again at the China-Kyrgyzstan border in three weeks. I feel I've known her for a long time.

Utkir is our guide now, in Uzbekistan, and he is another story. His appearance is sloppy, his behaviour clearly indicates bored-with-life, and his manner is snarly and condescending. Especially toward women. He doesn't endear himself to Lynne and me. In an arrogant monotone, he tells us that his great-grandfather was a rich and powerful trader who travelled along the Silk Road, from his base in Samarkand to Iran and Palestine. We are not especially convinced nor impressed. I want Utkir to tell us what living in Uzbekistan is like now.

"My wife follows my instruction," he says curtly, coming back to the land of the living. "The behaviour of women is despicable in Uzbekistan but not as bad as in Iran." I feel close to Afghanistan now, and I won't push Utkir. Lynne's and my pain will be to listen to his rants about women. Ross and Bill wisely ignore him.

I will myself to shut down the whirlwind of disturbing thoughts about the life of women here and try to focus on the beauty of the moment as Ross and I walk through a sandstone twin-turreted gate into the city. The night is still, and the old city of Khiva is quiet, wrapped in ancient mystery. An immense silver moon floats up into a deep blue blanket of stars and casts its light over jewelled blue-green minarets and domes. I am not disappointed.

I sleep well.

Utkir says he's tired this morning, and to his credit, he has hired another guide, Guila, to be with us. The pristine, narrow winding streets of Khiva are devoid of life other than a few people trying to sell souvenirs. There are no cars and no tourists. A hot desert wind shifts briskly about massive sun-baked mud walls circling for three kilometres around centuries-old fortresses, residences, palaces, mausoleums, mosques, and bazaars. Guila's pretty long yellow silk dress and matching head scarf swirl about as she articulates, in careful English, life as it was, and is now, inside the ancient walls. Her face conveys an ethnicity different from others living here. Mongolian perhaps, and although it expresses a warm personality and intelligence, it seems to hold some pain or secret. Her arms, hands, head, and eyes move to emphasize every word, and she is pleased that Lynne and I ask questions about her family.

She's thirty-eight years old and met her husband when they were both studying foreign languages in university. "We have three children, two boys and a girl, and we live with my mother-in-law. She's eighty-five years old and she's my fourth child," Guila laughs. "In our culture, the youngest son must always look after his parents, and my husband is the youngest."

The mother of the youngest son is lucky to have such an outgoing, happy daughter-in-law, I think to myself. When I ask if there are many women who are guides, she says, "No. But there are two carpet factories and a ceramic factory in Khiva where many women work."

Later I learn that Guila is Hazara, a people descended from the Mongol invaders along the Silk Road. They speak a Persian dialect and follow Shiite Islam. The women are active, visible in public, and often well educated. Because they are not Pashtun or Sunni, they suffer from discrimination, especially in Afghanistan, where many Hazars live. Could this be the pain I note in Guila's face? We met each other only a few hours ago, and these are questions I cannot yet ask. I'm sorry I can't spend time here, to be like a fly on the wall in Guila's life and to savour what it is like for her.

158

I have found a cool, shady spot in the courtyard of the Great Mosque in Bukhara to sit alone and write. The colours of sand are all around me, embedded in the magnificence of whitewashed walls, sandstone walkways, and breathtaking cobalt-blue and turquoise tiles. The imam walks across the empty courtyard that is big enough for 10,000 people to kneel and pray in. He is an elegant figure; his dark robes shift to offset brilliant sunshine. In spite of the impressive Islamic architecture, I feel uneasy. An air of religious sterility surrounds me. There are few veils covering faces, no calling to prayer five times a day from the minarets. The mosques are open and charge admission for tourists to enter. I ask myself, is this a relic of the Soviet antireligion era? Is Islam here a guise to ratify power and control? What is lurking behind the control, the hidden information, and the power figures?

My new friend, Ortinoy, sits beside me. An olive-skinned, scrawny, four-foot-tall girl in a scruffy short dress, she radiates exuberance. When I first met her last evening while I walked around the town, she told me she's thirteen years old and is on her summer vacation. She's in grade seven.

"I am an independent girl," she laughed. "All children born after Independence Day, September 1, 1991, we call independent kids." She is one of seven children. "Who's the boss in your family?" she asks abruptly.

Wow. This girl can read minds. I might have asked her the same question. Instead, I stall and say, "Well, now. In our family, there are two bosses. Ross and me."

"My father is the boss in my family. Not really. Sometimes

it's my mother. My mother buys the pottery and I sell it. I can speak twelve languages."

Her English is perfect, and as she rattles off examples of other languages she speaks, I have no doubt she speaks twelve languages. And that it is she who is the boss in her family.

"Do you learn all these languages in school?"

"No. We don't learn anything in school. We learn it from the tourists. I want to be a guide when I grow up."

"When will you graduate from school?"

"Grade nine. I'm saving my money for university. I am going to study foreign languages."

There are few tourists in Bukhara today. I am told it is because of the weather now. Too hot, they say. I think back to our visa fiasco and the news about the massacre three months ago in Uzbekistan, in Andijan, not far from here. I hope the tourists will come again. For Ortinoy's sake.

Scrub desert, the disastrous remains of cotton monoculture, flank the black, hot asphalt highway from Bukhara to Samarkand. Definitely not the golden road of my dreams. We take a short detour and get out of the van for a couple of hours to visit Timur the Lame's birthplace, Shakhrisabz. Timur was a ruthless warrior who, in a nine-year rampage, laid Iran, Iraq, Syria, eastern Turkey, and the Caucasus at his feet. If not for him, we wouldn't be going to Samarkand today. He was a patron of the arts, and he poured all his plundered riches into what became his brilliant golden capital.

Finally, in the heat of the afternoon, we arrive in the

outskirts of the city and drive through narrow streets to a small inn with a pleasant, busy courtyard. I'm happy to finally stop, rest, and sip gin and tonic with friends. The evening is still; a slight breeze rustles dry leaves in giant plane trees outside the courtyard wall. Dogs bark, roosters crow, birds sing, soft voices murmur.

My thoughts drift back to Bukhara.

I've figured out that my young friend and her girlfriends in Bukhara cheated me when they sold me that special little piece of pottery her aunt made by hand. She charged me way too much, and the pottery is stamped "China."

They also terrorized Ross. I wasn't there, but he tells me a pack of girls led by Ortinoy surrounded him when he was sketching in the mosque. They tore at him trying to force him to buy their trinkets.

Ortinoy yelled, "By the time I finish trying to sell you this, you are going to wish you'd bought it in the first place."

"She had transformed from a nice little kid into a hellion," Ross tells us. "Eventually," my kind and gentle husband says, "I was able to break away."

I am shaken. What is the future for children like Ortinoy?

I try to defend her and say, "Ortinoy will be a powerful leader."

"In the drug business," Ross says. "Now they run the drugs, not silk, from Afghanistan to Uzbekistan and on to the West, and even Canada."

In 1965, when we travelled through Afghanistan, we had other issues to deal with, and for us, the drug trade was not known. Now it has consumed not only political structures but the social fabric as well. Countries are crumbling. People like Ortinoy have few choices, few channels for their gifts of being clever.

I can't deal with the thought of it. I throw out Ortinoy's pottery. So I can forget.

But it doesn't work. I can't forget.

We start exploring Samarkand early to beat the heat, but the sun is already baking as we go up the steep flights of stairs to Shah-i-Zinda, the tomb of the Living King, a cousin of the Muhammad who brought Islam to this area. The site, with the sparkling city sprawling below, was developed between the ninth and fourteenth centuries, before Timur the Lame's time. Could it have been this spot Marco Polo was thinking of when he wrote, "Samarkand is a large and splendid city"?

We climb hundreds of stairs crowded with pilgrims praying and stepping slowly around ritual buildings, mausoleums, and mosques; my heart reaches out to them. I think about what they may be praying for. Peace. Health. Food. A safe place to be. The same things I want for the world.

Samarkand's medieval commercial plaza, the Registan, is the favourite Central Asian tourist site and, some say, the most important. I am surprised there are not many people here. In the vast empty spaces, I have to work hard to imagine the time long ago when theology, astronomy, mathematics, and philosophy were taught in the immense gold-domed and blue-tiled madrassas. It was the centre of learning in Central Asia.

Little souvenir shops behind the plaza now fill the madrassas. They are lifeless and unsettle me. What am I supposed to be looking at here? Up at the domed mud-brick ceilings? Around at the crumbling blue-tiled walls? In that corner at the sleepy shopkeepers? Over on that table, at the made-in-China souvenirs?

Where is Ross? There he is. In the far corner of the plaza, sketching quietly, ignoring the people around him. I can see that he wants to savour the magnificence of this city on the fabled golden road on his own terms. Ross has now wisely opted out of touring and shopping.

A master of ignoring onlookers while he draws, Ross is immersed in the remarkable architectural accomplishments. Samarkand's mythical and turbulent history explodes in larger-than-life monuments Timur and his grandson built in the fifteenth century. These are the monuments the Russians restored and rebuilt in the twentieth century.

But for me Samarkand has been reduced to a lifeless jumble of architectural masterpieces (I should have paid more attention to the clues in Fletcher's pristine drawings in *A History of Architecture*). I am struck by the gap between the Samarkand I longed to see and the big empty square surrounded by perfectly Russian-restored antiquities and tacky contemporary structures.

It is true that "we travel not for trafficking alone . . . but for lust of knowing what should not be known. . . . our fiery hearts are fanned." Perhaps Ortinoy's story has put me off track. But knowing and understanding Samarkand remains elusive to me.

I need to leave and find something fresh. Something to see that I'm alive.

Urgut is a small town forty miles from Samarkand, up a winding gravel road into the hills to the south, near Afghanistan. It is cool in the mountains, and the fresh air is a relief from baking asphalt streets.

"This is a great idea, Ross. Look at that scenery. Fabulous." I ache to get out into the crisp mountain air to hike, but I can't. It's not safe. This is one of Uzbekistan's main drug-growing areas, and we probably would be shot. Or kidnapped. I knew this when I balked at Ross's idea.

"Before we leave Uzbekistan, we should try to get out into the countryside, where the handicrafts are made and sold. The market at Urgut is the busiest and most colourful in the area," Ross told us. Then, seeing the horror in my eyes, he continued with a savvy grin, "You and Lynne can probably find better-quality handwork there than the cheap stalls around the Registan in Samarkand."

I think back to our visits to the bazaar in Kabul where we bargained for the small carpet that is so much a part of our lives now. I'm glad we spent one of our last dollars on it. Every day it helps me connect to the lives of women who live there. I'm keen to forget the danger and repeat the market experience.

We finally get out of the van on a dusty, busy street. We weave our way through rows of stalls jammed with people and carts loaded with goods to sell. Children, squealing with happiness, run in and out of the rows of stalls, with sheep baa-ing, chickens squawking, and donkeys braying. We work our way through masses of modern goods — pots, televisions, and cellphones: you name it, and it's here.

And then suddenly we stumble on the place we have been looking for. Stalls piled with bolts of silk, wool, cotton, fur, and leather.

Central Asia is a land of textiles. For centuries, women here have spun, dyed, woven, and embroidered just about everything they use at home.

Sellers crowd around us. A woman in a flowing black robe, a chador, in the Persian style, approaches us carrying an armful of cheap polyester scarves. Made in China. Probably. She works hard to catch my eye.

"New or old," she cries. "Cheap. Cheap. How much you want to pay?"

Like Ortinoy, she knows our language. I struggle to keep my eyes diverted. If I make eye contact, I know I will begin the bargaining process. I don't need any more polyester scarves.

Bill says, "But they're desperate to sell, Nancy." He struggles not to buy, but he wants to, to help. There are a lot of peddlers but no other tourists. Have they been frightened away by the political and revolutionary fiascos?

Hanging from the ceiling in the corner of a stall at the back of the market is a large decorative piece of fabric, different from all the rest. I try to control myself. Submerge my squeals of delight. Abide by the principles of expert

165

bargaining. I fail.

The merchants working in the stall, expert bargainers, carefully take it down for me. They know what the wonder in my eyes means for them.

Rough brown cotton is heavily sewn with fine satin and chain-stitch swirls in shades of pink and turquoise. Each loop is unique. A wavy cream embroidered line around the perimeter embraces the swirls. What is your story? I silently ask of the artist who sewed the piece so long ago.

"It's very special," the market ladies say, gathering around. They too admire the piece. "This is an antique *suzani. Suzani*, in our Persian language, means needle. Look at the fine stitching," the stall boss lady says. "Our language is Persian. This *suzani* was made for a dowry, over a hundred years ago. Now we are selling it."

The survival of beautiful handwork like this helps people appreciate the lives of women—it tells their story, pictures their lives in yurts, tents, and villages. Their handwork gives them status and helps answer questions. Does it describe a prosperous family, an anticipated marriage, an important life journey? Does it celebrate a birth?

The *suzani* I buy will give a woman somewhere extra income to support her family. For a little while.

Calgary, April 29, 2009. I am treated to a little surprise this morning as I pick up my *suzani* to think about how I can write about it. "HH.TUKKEHMARAT" is stitched into the creamy right-hand border. I don't know what it means. This is the first time I've noticed it. But it is a special gift that helps me explore another world.

my horse and me crossing a high pass, kyrgyzstan, 2005

XV

feeling free (CHINA, KYRGYZSTAN)

OURNAL ENTRY, August 6, 2005. "This trip isn't the quiet, spiritual experience I'm looking for in Central Asia. The edges are hard. Long drives across earth raped by cotton monoculture are broken by stops in ancient cities packed with gold domes and blue-tiled architectural masterpieces. I try to ignore our guide, Utkir, who has a hard, mean soul. I feel an oppressive control here, a controlled political simmer, ready, at any time, to boil over. I can hardly wait to get to be free again."

It was a relief to safely cross the border out of Uzbekistan into Kyrgyzstan's fertile Fergana Valley. We chose to cut across Kyrgyzstan before taking a short loop into China to visit the fabled city of Kashgar. Our guides from the Kyrgyz community-based tourism company were waiting at the border to take us to spend the night in the village of Sary Tash at the east end of the Irkeshtam Pass. At first, from the garden of our yurt home-stay, we couldn't even see the Pamir Range in the Himalayas to the south. Then someone said, "You have to look up. Way up. Over the clouds." And there was Mount Lenin, 7,134 metres high.

Our start tomorrow is at 3:00 a.m. to get across the border before it closes at noon.

Contrary to what guidebooks say, the pass up through Irkeshtam is a miserable dirt track with bathtub-size potholes. This "new highway" is an Uzbek-Kyrgyz-China project to revitalize old trade routes between China and Central Asia. In the cold dark morning, at the speed of a lame donkey, I am jolted around in all directions in the back of a noisy van crammed with spare tires, suitcases, and six tired bodies. The whiff of coffee gently percolating at home is only a dream; whiffs of diesel are my new reality. With every giant pothole manoeuvre, our plan to visit romantic Kashgar becomes more elusive and our sanity is challenged.

Then, silently, the sky morphs from black to pink and gold, framing snowcapped peaks towering all around us. I can see Marco Polo and his entourage charging across the rock-strewn pass with the magnificent glaciated Tian Shan Mountains in the north and rugged tops of the Pamirs to the south.

I know why I want to be here now — to walk in their footsteps.

But I'm brought back to reality when our driver snaps, "Trekking is not permitted. We need to get you to the border before it closes." Marco is put on hold.

The border grates me, with its massive rolls of barbed wire and officious teenage soldiers strutting about with machine guns slung across their crisp green uniforms. They are anxious for action as they flip aggressively through our passports. I struggle to control my fear — and my identity.

"That's my passport. I could be your grandmother," I say to try to be sociable. They don't get it. As with border guards everywhere, being friendly is not the job.

The soldiers insist that the big Chinese transport trucks, carrying loads of used iron between Kyrgyzstan and China, are the only vehicles permitted to drive across the disputed twenty-kilometre stretch of land between the two countries. They will arrange for us to hitch a ride in a truck. The rule is one hitchhiker per truck.

"But look," I plead, pointing to my friend Lynne, "we're grandmothers. We can't hitchhike alone." The boss soldier looks at us strangely. He can't figure out why we're here among dishevelled drivers and mechanics waving their wads of documents, trying to get their trucks through to China.

"You two. Together. The men. Separate," he barks.

It's a struggle for Lynne and me. In many ways. We leave our husbands behind the barbed wire. We pull and heave our suitcases (damn, why did I buy those rugs and fur hats in Bukhara?) into the high rear end of our designated mammoth trailer truck. We hoist our not-getting-any-younger bodies up a steep ladder and squeeze our sweating, breathless selves into the cab beside the driver.

Tea is waiting. A well-muscled but kind-looking Chinese man about forty hands us his scraped and worn water bottle filled with cold green tea. We nod in thanks, he nods, and then in silence we drive to the Chinese border without incident.

"Welcome to China," says the sign over a sleek, modern customs and immigration building where our Chinese guide is waving to us.

We wait hours for Ross and Bill.

Ross finally arrives and regales us with his story. His truck broke down in the middle of no-man's land; he walked, dragging his suitcase behind him for a few kilometres, between antiaircraft guns and barbed wire alongside the road, before he could find another truck to hitch with.

Sometime later, Bill arrives and hesitantly tells us how a soldier pointed a gun at him and demanded money. Our sweet and kind Bill gave him ten bucks. "This money is for your kids," Bill told him.

The Silk Road city of Kashgar is now a modern, dirty one, with lots of traffic, but its mosque is an escape for me to sit and think about connections—the Uzbeks, Uighurs, Kyrgyz, Koreans, Russians, Mongols, and Han Chinese who have come together here for centuries. To get a more realistic flavour of the importance of this historical Silk Road junction, we decide to drive out of town along the old route and then take camels into the desert.

The Taklamakan "Desert of Death" is one of the largest and most inhospitable sand wastelands in the world, and its oases were important market towns that could determine the success of a trading venture.

We meet our camels and a cheerful camel herder–guide and his family in a little settlement. They're keen to have tourists stop by and are ready to help us. My camel kneels down, I scramble onto her saddle of colourful handmade blankets, and she leans forward on her front haunches, lurching herself, and me, up, backsides first.

For as far as I can see, from my perch several feet above the desert, there is nothing but drifting sand and dunes.

We pad across the desert in silence as dark clouds gather in the north and a dangerous cold wind blows in. Small sand cyclones swirl around, blinding for a moment. The winds of the Taklamakan are notorious, and I've read about people who have ventured out into this desert, never to return. Perhaps Marco Polo would have kept on going through the brewing storm to the next oasis several days away, but I'm happy to be led back to the settlement and the herder's home for a cup of tea.

The camel trip is just enough to reignite my imagination of what travelling along the Silk Road could be like. I can't wait to go back through the mountains and over the Torugart Pass, to Kyrgyzstan and, like Marco, get on my horse.

Zamira is waiting for us, smiling and waving, when we get across the border.

"Welcome back to Kyrgyzstan," she says.

We drive through a tight green velvet valley in the At-Bashy Range of the Tian Shans and stop awhile at Tash Rabat, a small fifteenth-century caravanserai. Crumbled walls corroborate its history of traders spending the night safely here, perhaps, like me, embellishing their stories of travel.

A group of Kyrgyz horsemen with half a dozen dishevelled French clients rides into the village. They're the first tourists we've seen in days, and we're all eager to share adventures. The young Frenchmen say they're exhausted but are obviously thrilled with their adventure as they boast about their horse-trekking escapade across Kyrgyzstan.

"We're on our way to camp beside Lake Song-Kul too," I tell them. "It's at 3,016 metres. Then we drive to Lake Issyk Kul to pick up our horses at Shepherd's Way Trekking before we start our long ride across the mountains. Do you think we'll make it?"

Horrified disbelief flashes across their young faces, and they shrug a silent answer.

The wind tears around the grassy steppe, circles the lake, and screams up the gullies between rounded hills. The air is fresh; the sky is blue. The only sign of human habitation is a neat group of six yurts, an outhouse, and a corral with a dozen or so horses. A thin twirl of smoke and the faint aroma of dinner stewing rise from the largest yurt.

"We call it god's country and come here every year for a vacation together," says one of three women who come to greet us. They're sisters, they tell us, and those seven lanky teenagers roaring around the yurts, some on muscular Kyrgyz horses, others kicking soccer balls around, are their children.

At dinner, we all sit together on hand-sewn carpets around a long table, and I note in awe that the eighty-year-old grandmother sits down cross-legged with ease and grace. Sitting on the floor at a low table is not easy. Silently I vow to practise my Kyrgyz-table-sitting position when I get home to Canada and my daily yoga.

The sisters explain that one of them now lives in America, one lives in Paris, and one still lives in Kyrgyzstan. We don't need to explain where Calgary is; they know the 1988 Olympics. Toasts are proposed.

"We are thankful to be here all together with our sisters and their families and our new Canadian friends."

"We too are thankful to be here in your lovely country, at this memorable place with you." I speak slowly, trying to mimic their formality. "We are honoured to meet you and your children." I want to stay and be with this beautiful family longer, but we leave early tomorrow morning for Barskoon village, where our week of horse trekking will begin.

Barskoon village is on the shore of Lake Issyk Kul, the fourth-deepest lake in the world, and we'll rest here for part of the day before we pack for tomorrow's start of the horse trek. I'm happy to lie here in my sleeping bag and look out at blue sky through the opening in the roof and listen to the sounds of morning — roosters crowing, wood being chopped, donkeys braying, birds singing.

I think of the yurt as a model of our world. The form has been developed over centuries, a practical place for families to live. Full of symbolism and beauty, our yurt is more than a tent. Its thick, unbleached white felt covers a round bent-willow lattice frame so, traditionally, it can be packed easily and carried on horseback to the next pasture. The ornamentation may have had its origin in designs of the Bronze Age, but most decoration today is inspired by indigenous natural elements. The interior colours are cheerful, strong, and contrasting. Piles of wool blankets, stacked around the edges during the day, are patched and embroidered in patterns that reflect sympathy with the earth, mountains, water, and stars. As with other handwork in Central Asia, sometimes the craftswoman sews in coded messages, messages to last generations.

Stylized ram's horns, *kochkor*, popular motifs in Kyrgyzstan, are appliquéd onto handcrafted colourful *shyrdaks*, felt rugs that cover the floor of our yurt. Our door is decorated with handmade tassels and ornaments that symbolize power and prosperity. Outside, ram's horns over the door protect us. Black and white yakhair tassels hang around the exterior of the tent to keep us from the evil eye and, hopefully, extend the safety element to us while we're on our horse trek.

Almost as if to set the scene for a movie production, under the apple tree next to our yurt is a large golden eagle tethered to a wooden perch. Beside the eagle, on a greying white plastic lawn chair, sits an old man with a beautiful smile and a sunburnt, weathered face. He tells us his job is to train the eagle.

"It's important," he says, "because we almost lost our nomadic traditions in Kyrgyzstan when the Russians ruled." Falconry has been a traditional sport of nomads in the Central Asian steppes for thousands of years. To experience falconry, I get fitted with long, thick leather gloves, then call the magnificent thrashing bird to perch on my skinny arm.

It may sound easy, but it isn't. I scratch falconry off my to-do list.

"Remember. Trust your horse," Gulmira, the co-owner

of Shepherd's Way Trekking, yells down the gully as she waves goodbye.

So I do. We are going to ride from the inside to the outside of the Tian Shan Mountain range. Carefully, we descend the cliff and cross the river.

I love the steady pace of my Kyrgyz horse, Salat (or Roan, in English, the colour of its grey speckled coat). His pace is slower than other Central Asian breeds and he's a little smaller, 13.5 hands—just right for me. Domesticated even before Mongolian horses were, the Kyrgyz horse has been on the central steppes of Asia for over 4,000 years, and today he's part of Kyrgyzstan's cultural heritage and the identity of nomads and shepherds.

Salat's superb agility keeps me safer than my own two feet would as we ride up and down high mountain pastures, over narrow rocky passes, and down through pine forests. He deftly picks his way through roaring streams. Kyrgyz horses are strong and keep in good shape, even on long treks, when fodder may be scarce. I'm happy to note that they also are able to scare away wolves.

Blankets of wildflowers, gentian, forget-me-not, and wild geranium cover the earth. I remind myself to find out someday why nature appears to put like colours together in one chosen area—the orange, the red, the pink. Beyond a knoll and its wildflower garden, 5,000-metre peaks tower above and are reflected below in ice-blue Lake Issyk Kul at 1,600 metres. A soft blue haze across the lake softens the jagged caps of the Tian Shan range beyond.

I hear a roar coming from the thinnest of waterfalls in

the tiniest mountain stream. Is this the quiet at the top of the world?

We're not alone, though. Shepherds on horseback, poised in silhouette against the deep blue sky, patrol thousands of grazing sheep and cattle. They carry not much more than a pair of binoculars slung across their shoulders. When they catch sight of us, they hurtle down the mountain, leap off their horses, and vigorously shake hands with the men. Young and ruddy-complexioned, they flash their gold teeth and laugh uproariously when I say that in Canada women shake hands too.

They tell me they're here with their families for the summer. They've driven the livestock from their village to fresh pasture and camp in the yurts that dot the hillside. Each evening, they corral their animals to protect them.

"Big problem. Predators," one man says. "Wolves, fox, bear, lions."

I remind myself to sleep lightly, listen for the lions, and hope my horse keeps the wolves away.

Murland, our horse guide, is leading us over another stony pass "to the outside" of the mountain range. We have been inside. I hardly know which is which. The pass is long and high, up a narrow rocky gorge. *Clop, clippity, clippity clop. Ping, bang, bang. Bang.* Rockfalls, waterfalls, and snowfalls, the avalanches, do not deter us. When we reach the top of the pass and look over to the outside—that feels like the inside to me—we can see a clear, rock-bottomed river cutting through a wide green valley below. We stop beneath the towering peaks that surround us. To our surprise, a young bearded man with a backpack rides toward us on a mountain bike. He stops and tells us, briefly, he's Israeli and has biked all the way from Jerusalem to explore his roots. Then he gets back on his bike and rides away. I'm stunned. How curious life is. What are his stories? I ask myself.

"Yaks," says Murland in his quiet way. There in the distance is a herd of a hundred or so black and brown yaks and one huge white yak. Some have calves. Young men on horseback move around inside the herd. Prized for their thick fur coats, yaks are valuable animals for fibre, milk, and meat, and they thrive in these harsh highlands of Central Asia.

The "yak man's" yurt is a few feet from the place we choose to camp for the night, and as soon as we settle we have a visitor. He's a handsome figure in black leather riding pants, a long dark green corduroy jacket, and the inevitable binoculars hanging around his neck. His smile is warm and infectious. He's careful, of course, not to make eye contact with Lynne and me, the women.

"This is our tradition," our guides interpret. The yak man must always come to the visitors' "home" tent to greet them, give them a piece of bread and salt, and visit over a cup of tea. He talks about his yak herd that is owned by different people who live down in the village.

It is difficult to describe the awe I feel—this beautiful place, untouched and unspoiled. I find a huge pink granite rock covered with rust and grey lichen to sit on and scratch a few words in my journal. Ross has his own rock. His travel journal is a treasure of drawings, interesting words, and tiny sketches. He glues in wildflowers and assorted cutouts from souvenir papers and cards.

Tomorrow is our last day. Our horses are saddled and ready to go. They too are making the most of these last moments, munching green grasses before we all descend the Keregetash River gorge and make our way back to "the inside."

A jet flies low overhead. It is odd. We haven't seen a village or villagers for days, and now there's a jet.

"What's that plane doing here?" I ask.

"Military," says Murland. I am reminded of our arrival in Bishkek and seeing the huge American fighter jets lining the runway. There is, after all, a war going on not far away.

"Reconnaissance," I guess.

"At night?" asks Lynne.

"You know, infrared and all that spy stuff."

"You mean they're looking for Osama bin Laden here?"

"Maybe. It's not far."

God. Now gunshots.

Ross thinks it's a .22 or .303, whatever that is.

"Shooting wolves, I suppose," someone says.

And I am brought back to feeling free and the risks of being inside the world that is outside this outside.

teaching me falconry

ladies performing in hankou

XVI

connections (HANKOU, CHINA)

*T*HE SMILING BUDDHA is grinning at me from its place on the shelf above my computer. In 1920, my grandmother brought the porcelain figure from China to her new home in Toronto, and I rescued it a few years ago after my family abandoned it. Its shimmering coat, delicately painted face, and good-natured smile intrigue me now as they did when I was about the height of the railing in my grandparents' house. In those days, I would secretly visit the Buddha at its place in the small alcove where the stairs turned the corner. I would pick up its heavy, slippery body and hold it on my knee, like a doll. The Buddha was my friend, and we talked about the world.

Playing with my grandmother's Buddha was my practise ground for living in a complex world. It is my first memory of fascination with people and places far away. Especially China.

"I'm writing about the Buddha," I said when Sarah phoned last night and asked how I was getting along in my workshop at the Banff Centre.

"No, Mom. Your Buddha?"

She thinks I've gone off the deep end. She knows I'm in over my head here.

A silence slips around the uncertainty in our conversation as it often does in discussions when we don't immediately connect and are puzzled by where the talk will go. Then gales of laughter break the quiet as we remember the time I brought the Buddha home to my family in Calgary.

I could not explain then what the Buddha meant to me.

"It doesn't belong here," they said.

"How did you get it?"

"Where did it come from?"

"Don't put it there!"

And so it was banished to my tiny upstairs office that fills with morning sun. It could not have found a better home. From a perch above my computer, my Buddha tells me, "Write down your stories."

Why am I telling you this now? My Buddha helps me move into another space, another world, so that I can write.

October 2002. There are two other Caucasians on this sparkling new Boeing 737 China Southern Airline flight. The plane groans and grinds as we settle into a brisk descent. The sun's brilliant light breaks through a thick grey blanket, and the earth below me changes. Green checkerboard fields stretch as far as I can see. Like a lace tablecloth, convoluted grey and brown lakes spread over the landscape. Channels connect, dikes crisscross, great muddy rivers twist. Boats silently slink along waterways.

My heart is pounding. What lies before me seems familiar. Have I been here before?

Look. There is the Chang Jiang, the Yangtze River, with its fertile flood plain. And there is Hankou, the city where my grandparents came to live almost a hundred years ago. They told their children stories about it, and my father told the stories to me. So, yes, in a way that stories are part of us, I have been here before.

It is not difficult to understand the awe Marco Polo felt in the thirteenth century when he first travelled the river I see below. He was searching for an efficient route to take silk back to Europe. Even in those days, it surprised him to see the tremendous volume of traffic and trading along the Chang Jiang.

Like Marco Polo, Grandfather was an adventurer and a merchant. He took his young family to China to look for a way to export silk and other materials for making hats to New York and Europe.

I want to understand the China my grandparents went to. How did the China of 1910 to 1920 come to be?

Centuries before Marco Polo arrived, the Song Dynasty (960–1126) renewed Confucian principles that determined conduct, patterns of obedience, and governance. Central administration was reinstated. Advances in land reclamation, farm technology, and rice production encouraged growth and began the development of a strong merchant class.

Trade between China and Europe started in the mid-1500s, when the Portuguese set up a walled enclave in Macao, off the southeast coast. Then the Dutch, British, and French came, and by the end of the Ming Dynasty, in the mid-1600s, Hankou, on the north bank of the great Chang Jiang, was one of China's main commercial centres.

Foreigners needed tea, silk, porcelain, and other products. The Chinese, with a diverse economy, needed only gold, and so gold poured out of Europe. To balance trade, Europeans desperately searched for a commodity that China wanted, and eventually they found a hook: opium. Addiction to the drug grew quickly in China. The flow of gold reversed, flooding back to Europe.

The Qing Dynasty struggled to gain control of the situation. The Opium Wars began in 1840 when the Chinese burned 20,000 chests of opium belonging to the Europeans. It is no surprise that the Europeans fought back. The dynasty weakened terribly, so as a last resort, to save itself from annihilation, the Qing signed a treaty with the Europeans in return for withdrawal of all foreigners from the area around Peking. International concession areas were permitted in four main commercial cities far away from the capital. Hankou was one of them.

Unfortunately, the treaty that the Chinese signed did not solve their problems. Hatred of the foreigners in China grew, fuelled by the country's fast-growing population, scarcity of arable land, and inability of Westerners, including missionaries, to connect with the hearts of the Chinese people. The dynasty tried to ride out the tide of antiforeign sentiment and sided with bands of poorly organized nationalist revolutionaries, the Boxers. Finally, China declared war on foreign powers in 1900.

They were promptly defeated.

To make matters worse, the Dowager Empress died in 1908, and a two-year-old boy ascended the throne. About the same time, provincial leaders in China were revolting over the question of foreigners owning the new railway between Wuhan and Peking.

Trouble continued. In October 1911 the revolutionaries accidentally exploded a bomb in Hankou, and their leader, the charismatic Dr. Sun Yat-sen, then in exile, was forced to return to lead more action against the Qing Dynasty. Sun Yat-sen and the revolutionaries gained control sooner than they expected and then needed to find a diplomatic way to persuade the emperor to abdicate. They engaged the former leader of the Qing military to mediate the process.

It did not work.

It was an uncertain time in China. However, in uncertainty there is also possibility, and there was hope of a better future for China.

About this time, my grandparents arrived in Hankou from my grandfather's workplaces in New York and Le Havre, France.

❧

A small young woman about twenty years old in blue jeans and a skintight pink T-shirt pushes through the crowd of greeters and easily spots Ross and me in the mass of disembarking passengers.

"Hello. My English name is Wendy. I will be your guide," she says briskly. Her efficiency disturbs me as she grabs our arms, pushes us forward through the throng of well-wishers at the gate and throws our suitcases into the sleek black taxi waiting for us.

"Today we are lucky," she says. "It has been raining for weeks."

Between tall dikes that brake the muddy Yangtze, our car races along the thirty-kilometre superhighway toward the city. Water buffalo forage in swamps along the way. Buses, trucks, VWs, Audis, Peugeots, and no-name taxis blast their horns, squeal their wheels, and belch their fumes as they speed beside us. We fly past men, women, and entire families on bicycles decorated with colourful paper streamers. They remind me of my bike as a child, on Victoria Day. Young and old men strain to pull rusted, creaking rickshaws overflowing with grain, vegetables, and fruit. Streams of people walk quickly along the dikes, some in Western dress, jeans, and T-shirts, others clothed in dark, more traditional-looking outfits, loose Chinese trousers, and neat-collared Mao-type jackets.

Packed forms — boxes, triangles, and giant golf balls on giant pillars — the skyscrapers, steal their way up through thick black smog. Crumbling French colonial buildings struggle to stay upright and alive. Everywhere clothes hang

188

on worn overhead wires and frayed ropes. Dust and diesel fumes permeate the air. People jam the streets.

Not to be defeated, our taxi honks and blasts its way through crowded, grungy alleys.

"Not many tourists go out of their way to Hankou," I read in my guidebook.

Strangeness and disorder consume me, and I have to work hard to hold on to the reasons I have come to Hankou. Then I remember my Buddha, its cheeky smile and its beckoning me to settle in and look for answers to my questions about the past that has made the present.

Chattering nonstop in disconnected English phrases, Wendy tries to tell us about Hankou. We grasp the facts. Hankou, Wuchang, and Hanyang are three convergent cities on two sides of the Yangtze that make up the mega-metropolis of Wuhan, the capital of Hubei province. Over fifty-eight million people live here, and the economy is thriving.

Wendy doesn't answer questions. She doesn't want to. Or maybe she is unable to. But I can't give up my pursuit for answers. I try French and then flounder with a few words of Mandarin, but my queries about the foreign concessions in Hankou float past Wendy to empty space. Wendy is determined not to stray from her script that tells us about the Yellow Crane Pagoda.

We have already read the script in our guidebook. I am annoyed with Wendy's artificial enthusiasm. She barks out that the Yellow Crane Pagoda was destroyed during the Cultural Revolution in the 1960s and rebuilt a few years

189

ago. It is now the symbol for Wuhan.

I drift off and daydream about the two brass yellow cranes that my mother polished every Friday to grace the coffee table at our home in Quebec. Where are those cranes now? They must have meant something special for my grandmother because she brought them back from China to America. If they went to a garage sale, I'm sorry, I want to tell my Buddha.

Wendy's unintelligible chattering stops when the taxi clatters to a halt in the porte cochere outside the Jiang Han Hotel. The courtyard is silent. A striking, tall young man about our son's age, dressed in a formal red mandarin jacket and black pants, smiles and silently motions us into the foyer.

Thankfully, Wendy disappears.

Calmness settles over me. I feel I have been here before. The elegant hallways, the graceful carved mahogany furniture, the grand winding staircase with its massive wooden bas-relief depicting victory of some sort, signal that we are connecting with colonial times past.

The place I know as my grandfather's house in Toronto surrounds me. Cigar smoke chokes the air. Large oil paintings, like ours at home, with deep blues and greens, hang to portray French countryside. Imposing naked men cast in bronze stake their place around the foyer. Soft, comfortable furniture is arranged in relaxed settings. A string quartet plays Strauss waltzes in the corner.

But there are no Europeans, no Caucasians here. No one speaks French or English. Although the lounge is crowded,

I feel strangely apart.

I thought it was auspicious when I found the Jiang Han on the Internet a few months before we left on our journey. Renovated by a Hong Kong firm, the building beautifully preserves its former life as the French consulate in the centre of the international concession. When I told my father where we were planning to stay in Wuhan, he sent me a copy of his birth certificate.

It was issued over ninety years ago. In this building.

I can feel the presence of my grandmother. It is 1914. She strides purposefully through these halls desperately trying to obtain a birth certificate for my father. She is alone, with a one-year-old and a baby, my father, in tow.

Grandfather was sent to China to represent a French millinery company. Shortly after he arrived, before Father was born, Grandfather was conscripted by the French military to go back to Europe for a few weeks to help translate for the army and settle a dispute with the Germans.

It began like all wars do. It was to last three weeks.

My grandmother waited in Hankou for two years for my grandfather to return; it seemed the war in Europe would never end.

I touch my father's birth certificate that is in my pocket and feel my grandmother's struggle to protect her children in the face of great uncertainty. I see her stern, lean face, framed by a roll of dark hair drawn back behind her furrowed brow. A tentative smile softens hollow eyes with dark circles underneath. She balances her baby, my father, at arm's length on the desk in front of her.

It is 1915; the military leader appointed by Sun Yat-sen to negotiate abdication of the emperor accomplishes his mission and then surprises everyone by appointing himself emperor. The whole world, it seems, is in chaos.

"I cannot wait for China to settle and the Great War to end. I need to leave. I need to go home." And Grandmother, with two babies and a trunk full of her treasures from China, travels by ship across the Pacific, then by train across North America to Brooklyn, New York, where her parents live. She continues her journey, again by steamship, across the Atlantic to France to meet Grandfather.

We tentatively step out into the alleyways that surround our hotel to try to find our way to the river and take some pictures. Curious old photographs haunt me from their places in family albums. For decades, I have known my father's *amah*, his nursemaid. Her almond eyes connect with mine. Her tiny black and white triangular slippers bind broken smashed feet and hint of stories I do not know. Is she still here?

The pictures my grandparents brought back from Hankou are on my desk in front of me. I see crowds of people in tattered clothing jamming the streets, carrying huge sacks and baskets loaded with grain on their backs. Improvised one-story cardboard and wooden shacks line the alleys. Faces are pinched, drawn, and unsmiling. I remember my grandfather saying that he knew the Chinese people would rise up against the foreigners in their country. They were tired of being oppressed—beaten socially, emotionally, and physically.

"It can't last forever that way," my grandfather said. He foresaw the turmoil and the wars that were about to begin. Could he have foreseen how long it would take?

There is an aura of fortune and good health in the smiling faces that toss noodles, stir-fry vegetables, shine shoes, and greet us. Bicycles, rickshaws, makeshift shops, steaming woks, charcoal fires, tables, and stools jam the alleys. People step aside to make way for us, perhaps sensing my uneasiness in the crowd.

I want to reach out, to sit and "talk" with the rosy-faced women shining shoes in the alleys. We talk with hands and signals, and someone in the crowd that is gathering quietly gestures for me to sit down on the short stool that one of them has put beside me. A small woman dressed in navy trousers and mandarin jacket sits on her little shoeshine box in front of me and calmly places my foot on her lap. Then she expertly protects my socks, brushes the dirt off my shoes, cleans them with a white paste, and smoothes on a brown polish. She finishes the job with a soft rub and a pat. Her touch and gentle smile connect with mine.

We climb up a long flight of yellow brick stairs to see where they go and discover they are part of a dike that protects the city from the river and also shields a massive new park along the river from the chaos of the city. Today is the park's grand opening. Kites fly high in soft breezes—

dragons, snakes, frogs, and the ever-present Japanese cartoon cat with big eyes, Hello Kitty — to celebrate the occasion. Hundreds of children crouch over a long strip of white cotton several city blocks long to paint pictures about their favourite stories. With pride, parents and teachers peer over tiny bodies to admire the artwork.

Families of one child, two parents, and four grandparents, dressed in their best clothes, stroll around rose gardens and playgrounds where brass bands perform. I try to blend in, but I can't. People smile kindly and point me out to their children. It is odd to be so obvious, but I am beginning to enjoy the attention and the new role I have made for myself: Canadian ambassador.

Young and old come forward and say, in English, "Hello. Welcome to Wuhan."

"*Ni hao*," I reply, and our friendship begins.

I sit down quietly, alone in a small outdoor theatre beside the river, to rest, to watch, and think about families. I remember my grandfather telling me about the nuns walking the banks of the Yangtze every morning to collect the corpses of abandoned babies, mostly girls. The unofficial population of China is almost two billion people now. The government's one-child policy is an attempt to control population growth, but the birth rate of boys is too high. I begin to understand better that present practises are grounded in the past.

Some ladies about my age, in the seats below, beckon me. We understand each other's sign language, smiles, and gestures. They would like me to join them. They're part of a

traditional dance group, amateurs who are performing ancient routines to the soothing music of four-stringed lutes,
zithers, ceremonial trumpets, and gongs. They proudly
show me the costumes they have made. Long mandarin
jackets in brocades of every colour top flowing silk trousers. They pick the outfit they think will best suit me. I try
it on, and we all take pictures of each other. I feel close to
these women. Their babies, like mine, would have been
quite young during the Cultural Revolution of the 1960s
when Mao's Red Guards barbarically eliminated all forms
of art, religion, and academia. It must have been a difficult
time for my new friends. I understand now their passion for
preserving ancient art forms.

On the confusing walk back to the hotel for lunch, tack-
ling Chinese street signs and dead-end alleys, we come to
yet another obstacle. The alley is crammed with big, expensive cars.

"This is probably where the best place to eat in Hankou is," Ross says. "In fact, this must be where all the sen-
ior bureaucrats eat. Or the car dealers." He turns abruptly
toward the entry with the long red canopy.

A smiling, pretty hostess dressed in a long, slim, bright
red cheongsam, the traditional Chinese dress, greets us. She
seats us, tries to help with the menu, and eventually we
slip into a dialogue with eyes, smiles, and signals. We've
learned in China that the surest way to solve our choice-of-
food dilemma is to walk around and point. There is not an
empty seat in this grand two-story restaurant, so our choices
will be excellent. Nearly everyone joins in our fun and

enthusiastically competes with each other to demonstrate what they think is the finest dish in Hankou.

Will it be steamed fish, sautéed grated potatoes with onion, or smoked pork?

I can still taste the magic flavour of those sautéed grated potatoes with onions in Hankou.

I see a youngster about ten years old on the other side of the restaurant. His parents are pointing at us — I'm getting used to being pointed at now — and gently urging him to walk over to us. The boy beams a shy smile. His face is scrubbed; his black hair is sleek and shiny. From their table, his proud family watches him. He stops at our table, stands up straight clasping his hands in front of his chest, and says, "Hello. Welcome to Hankou. Where are you from?"

I learned today that the Chinese, when they ask "Where are you from?" expect you to say where your father was born. So I explain I am from Hankou too.

We are leaving Wuhan. The city and the Chang Jiang, the Yangtze, are below. I pick up my journal, a pen, and I write.

Lift the blanket
And uncover the stories
That tell how the world changes.

A checkerboard of people emerges
Because paths crisscross
And connections are made.
Some stages are convoluted

Some are silent
But words unravel
And stories can be told.

My story is simple now.
Channels connect
Rivers twist
Sun breaks through dark clouds
And the world changes.

hankou, 1914

my grandfather (second from left) near
the french consulate, hankou, 1914

the same building today

gu si temple, sichuan province

XVII

double happiness (CHINA AGAIN)

I remember the temple and the bridge
Passed before, hills and streams
That all seem to have lain
In waiting for me: flowers
And willows so warmly opening up
Their beauty in welcome; out on
The plains, smoke showed thin;
The last rays of sunlight lingered
On warm sands: then a traveller's
Worries ceased, for nowhere could
A better halting place be found.

FROM DU FU, SELECTED POEMS (ABOUT 750 AD)
TRANSLATED BY REWI ALLEY (FOREIGN LANGUAGES PRESS)

*I*T IS EARLY OCTOBER 2008, and we are travelling again, this time toward the mountains west of Chengdu to visit Gu Si, an ancient monastery. Women, men, and children riding motorized bicycles, fast-moving trucks, and high-end cars cram the roads. I don't know my cars, but I think I am in what is called a limo; at least it's black with comfortable, luxurious seats in the back where I am sitting between Ross and Jenli. It definitely is not our Beetle of forty-five years ago. We've upgraded our travel style.

Ross is travelling to photograph and write about two new temples in Sichuan. I am going along to feel China's history and listen to people's stories.

Our driver, Mr. Chow, focuses and frowns as I try to engage him in a version of exchange I've cultivated in China—not English and not Chinese, lots of smiling and head wagging.

"*Ha. Ha ha ha. Ha ha. Ha ha ha ha ha. Xie, xie.*" Our interpreter, Mr. Xu, Jenli's husband, is sitting beside Mr. Chow and is shouting into his cellphone. Though the people of Chengdu are renowned for being jolly and outgoing, it took me a few trips here to figure out that the *ha ha ha's* were a not Chinese version of laughter but mean "yes, yes." Mr. Xu is saying, "Yes. Yes. Yes, yes, yes. Thank you," to someone, somewhere in the world, as we zoom down long boulevards flanked by rose gardens, willows, ginkgos, and towering showy condominiums. Gated entrances to subdivisions boast "High Class Circle," "Swan Lake Park," "Perfume Garden," and "The Loft" in English for a glamorous effect.

The world of elegant boulevards and condos abruptly gives way to narrow, wet country roads, and now we are hurtling by rice paddies dotted with the pink, mauve, and blue of hundreds of umbrellas. Women, mostly, crouch under them, carefully tending a new crop.

The road gets muddier and the sky darkens. The world around me changes again, as it often does in China, and we splash alongside rows and rows of neat new trailers with blue roofs and shiny white aluminum siding with the United Nations logo stamped on them. I recognize the trailers from a visit along the Silk Road in 1999 to a disaster relief operation in Turkey. We learned a lot about earthquakes on that trip, but I had almost forgotten about the terrible disaster here five months ago until last night, when we settled into our room on the twenty-second floor of a sleek new hotel in Chengdu.

Ross pointed to the information on the back of the door and said, "We need to memorize this. It's a map of our floor. Here's our room. Here is the exit. We need to keep the emergency kit they've supplied at the bedside tonight. With the flashlight."

He is not the same carefree Ross of forty-five years ago. We've learned through the years to be prepared, but not necessarily both of us at the same time. We depend on each other to fill in the gaps. Ross seems to know what to do in case of another earthquake here.

He has reasons for being concerned. When he was here last May, a couple weeks after the earthquake, the building he was meeting in began to tremble. A crack opened on the wall. The engineer he was with said, "Don't worry. The main upheaval zone is closer to the mountains."

Those are the mountains we are headed to now, and now I have my own concerns.

We steadily motor into the hills, and the car snakes into a dark, thick forest of palm, bamboo, and other trees — all of them exotic and mysterious. The road becomes a brown, wet path and finally it goes no farther. A few ladies selling souvenirs are milling around small tables outside an immense, moss-covered gate that leads into a court, where Mr. Chow parks the car. I get out and start walking up the hill on a path where I am able to glimpse four or five tiled roofs beckoning me to the temples stepping up the mountain and squeezing into the forest, their graceful corners turning upward, as though reaching for light. Some are moss green, others gold, the colour that in history is restricted to emperors, like Marco Polo's Kublai Khan. I take a deep breath. My worries about earthquakes, mudslides, and the world in general melt away. I love being in this ancient monastery that we first visited last year.

Du Fu, the great Chinese poet, historian, and sage, travelled around here in the mid-700s, and I can almost feel his presence. He wrote about what was real for him then, and even today Chinese people know and love his work. I like to keep a translation of his poems close by and reread them for inspiration. "For nowhere could a better halting place be found," he writes.

Gu Si monastery was built and settled more than a thousand years ago and has had many resurrections through centuries of rebellion, war, and plundering. In dense wet forest above the temples there is supposed to be a special holy place with a strong magnetic field, so powerful that a magnetic compass is useless.

The new temple building, near the summit, replaces a structure that was gradually destroyed, between 1950 and 1984, by robbers and Red Guards who traded artefacts for food. To me it is a miracle that people, including monks, are travelling again in China to places that have been desecrated and so violently ruined during their lives.

What draws them here?

I sit down on a small granite wall in the corner of a courtyard where incense is smoking and flaming vigorously in a massive brass cauldron. The temple is home to Helping Buddha, the Buddha with hundreds of outstretched arms and hands. There is an orange tree in the corner; its delicate branches reach out for light. Monks, mostly friendly elderly men, drift by, soft orange robes swirling about their feet, covered with clean white socks and sandals.

I sit to rest and immerse myself in thoughts of what went on before my time.

Was Marco Polo here when he travelled around China? Possibly. I understand why he needed to choose what he wrote about and what to embellish. Sometimes I have to stretch my imagination to understand times past too.

Marco Polo got to China in 1274 and finally met the ruler, Kublai Khan, grandson of the great Mongol warrior Genghis Khan. Kublai was fascinated with Marco and his stories of adventure, and they became friends. Kublai Khan was busy trying to rule China from the capital, now Beijing, and had little time for travel. What he needed was an emissary, someone who could visit his immense domain for him, find out what was going on, and report back. Coincidentally,

Marco was looking for work. He was young, enthusiastic, and a proven, keen explorer. He got the job.

Although it is possible he was here at Gu Si, he didn't write about it. Not to let my readings about Marco defeat me 750 years after he was in China, I convince myself that Marco, like Du Fu years before him, must have stopped here too.

"*Ni hao. Ni hao ma,*" the monks and I say to each other.

I try to act like I am Chinese. It is a charade, of course.

"After all," I reassure myself, "Dad was born in China, so technically, in Chinese terms, that means I'm from China."

I'm learning that communication is more than verbal skill. I'm better at the "more than" part. Communication is being there, showing interest, and listening. Even if I don't understand the words, the faces, eyes, and smiles tell a story. Bodies have a language of their own.

The monk's faces, though smiling, are taut, drawn, and sallow. I feel a little uneasy, like I am in a hospital. One monk is particularly eager to explain. With his limited English and my limited understanding of Chinese, I begin to grasp his story. He came to Gu Si because he had liver cancer, and now his health has been restored. He says vegetarian food and what he calls "negative air" have cured him.

I don't know what negative air is. Could it be one of the reasons people hold on to spiritual places like Gu Si, like moss clings to the temple roofs and trees? Does the magnetic spot above the monastery draw them in, while they reach through a dark forest within themselves for light?

A tidy-looking woman with pure white hair, dressed conservatively in a maroon woollen overcoat, wanders over to meet me. Her eyes, almost vacant, widen and search my face as she starts to talk. Her cheeks are hollow; she has no teeth. Another woman about half her age, dressed in a neat, navy blue wool suit, rushes over to help her and me. She speaks English.

I introduce myself. "My name is Nancy. I am from Canada. My husband is up there," I point up the hill to the temple above. "He's taking pictures." I pull out my camera and demonstrate.

"Ah. Canada. We thought you were from here. But you are Chinese, are you not?"

"No. Thank you for the compliment, but I was born in Canada. I live near the Rocky Mountains." Surprisingly, my "being Chinese" charade has been successful.

"Not many foreigners come here. We live here."

"But why? I thought only monks live here. Are you also monks?"

They giggle. "I came here when I retired three months ago," the younger woman says. I prod her for more. "I didn't know what to do; my husband is dead, and my son has his own family. So I came here to sort out myself. I work as a receptionist. I receive visitors, talk with them, and tell them about the monastery. I'll make some tea for you and your husband, and we can sit and talk."

"And when did your friend come?"

"She's been here since 1984. Before anyone else came here. When she got here, the monastery was in ruins. She doesn't know exactly how old she is. Over eighty, we guess."

I am guessing now too, imagining what her life has been like. She was born about 1924, when China was in turmoil. Violent crime, prostitution, and opium smuggling were rampant. There was child slavery in factories, destitution and starvation in the streets. Foreign and Chinese factory owners ruthlessly suppressed labour strikes. Chiang Kai-shek and his Kuomintang were fighting to stop Mao and the Communist forces, who were seeking change.

By the time my new friend was in her teens, Japan had invaded China for the second time, and the "burn all, loot all, kill all" campaign made it one of the most brutal occupations in modern history. Then, in her early twenties, when the Japanese had been defeated, she lived through the Chinese Civil War. Finally, after years of struggle, the People's Republic of China was established with Mao at the helm.

Was it a time of triumph, elation, and hope for her? Was China different? Were the promises of change kept?

By the time she was thirty, China's Great Leap Forward program was trying to address the urgent problem of how to feed everyone. It was a huge failure, and China lurched into a famine of devastating proportions. Millions starved to death.

She survived. Did her family? What happened to her children?

In the 1960s, when she was in her forties, the Mao cult, the Red Guards, and the Cultural Revolution in China flourished. Nothing was sacred and no one escaped the horrors. After the death of Mao, in 1976, and the 1980 official proclamation that the Cultural Revolution was a catastrophe, leadership in China embraced a practical, more open approach to reform and modernization. Some urban workers and farmers took advantage of new policies and opportunities. They thrived.

I ask her, "Why did you come here then? Weren't things looking promising in China in 1984?"

She shrugs and does not want to talk anymore. Does she forget? Does she want to forget? Did she need a quiet forest escape?

Was she too drawn by the special magnetic forces and "negative air" at Gu Si?

I look for clues to the meaning of "negative air" in the dictionary. "Negative. Off-putting." Does "negative air" put off stressors?

We say our goodbyes, and alone I start climbing up the hill again, passing clockwise through the five temples, each with its unique courtyard and its own Buddha. I don't stop. I want to get to the top to see the new temple built over the ruins of an ancient imperial structure. Last year when we visited, the new temple was a mess of saws, hammers, nails, boards, wet mortar, and tacky paint.

At the top, I step gingerly through construction debris before I round a corner into a sunlit plaza. There above me, shining, is New Ancient Temple with its massive oxblood columns, delicately carved decoration, and painted gold roof. I can see the Great Golden Buddha, bathed in sunlight streaming through massive doors and high windows.

There's a gathering of noisy young adult visitors in the courtyard where enormous granite steps cascade down from the temple. I'm taken aback. I haven't seen other visitors today, and I'm confused for a moment by the ruckus. The young people signal to me, inviting me to join them. They tell me they're university students from Chengdu, and they're here for an outing.

They're happy to have someone to speak English with. "Come, try this game with us," one of them giggles shyly.

How can I resist?

I am with friends, playing a game that is new for all of us.

We stand below the stairs about twenty feet in front of a smooth, shiny granite wall that features a giant red Chinese character rimmed in gold: 喜. It is the character Double Happiness. We face it, and each in turn shut our eyes tightly, stretch out our arms, and stagger toward it to place our palms on the 喜. We all collapse with laughter and shout encouragements.

Happiness is elusive. But we keep trying. Eventually, focus and determination triumph, and we reach our goal.

I am thinking. Is our game in the New Ancient Temple symbolic of the story of the Chinese? Twist, turn, stagger through history, reach out, try and try again, focus. Touch the goal. Touch Double Happiness.

I know Mr. Chow is waiting for me at the base of the monastery, and since I haven't seen Ross, Mr. Xu, and his wife, Jenli, for a couple of hours, I start scrambling down the mountain on my own. On the way, I meet the three of them, who tell me that they've tried to find the special magnetic place farther up the mountain.

Mr. Xu laughs. "The story is true, but no one has actually been able to find it," he admits.

"But I've found Double Happiness," I boast. "Maybe that's why people come."

He whispers, widening his eyes and raising his eyebrows. "Yes, there're lots of reasons this place is very, very famous."

"But now we should eat," Jenli suggests. "Instead of scrambling around in the dirt up here, let's walk down to the bottom through the trees. This is the path that was the road in ancient times."

Although Mr. Xu is not an official interpreter, he speaks modest English and has known us for a few years now. He seems to understand us instinctively and we, him. He has brought Jenli on this excursion today because he knew we would enjoy each other's company, especially at mealtime.

Jenli has a beautiful, young, calm face and a slim, athletic body. She doesn't speak any English, but we seem to be able to read each other's thoughts. Smiling comes easily to her, and I am touched by her quiet awareness and appreciation of nature. She takes my arm and points into the woods. "Look at that. You know, this forest is very, very famous in China. It has hundreds of species of trees and birds."

Mr. Xu is translating. "My wife says she is so sorry she can't speak English. She says she wants to be able to speak to you directly. Next time, maybe she will have had time to learn English. Maybe I will teach her."

"No. No. Don't let your husband teach you," I fuss.

"Come visit us in Canada. Stay awhile. You'll learn English, and I'll learn Mandarin. We'll go hiking in our mountains; then when we go back to my house, we'll cook together. You can teach me how to cook Chinese, and I'll show you how to make roast beef and apple pie."

"But I have no time now. Maybe when I retire," she laughs.

I'm taken aback. "Retire? That won't be for a long time. You're too young." Shock waves run through me. I must have miscalculated. "What do you do?"

"I'm a doctor."

"What kind?"

"An obstetrician. I work at the Women's Hospital in Chengdu. This year is a milestone for me. I've been delivering babies for twenty-five years."

My brain races to imagine her history. She must have been born in the '60s and gone to school during the Cultural Revolution.

"We don't like to talk about those times," Mr. Xu says. "Almost everyone suffered. Now we put that behind us."

Nonetheless, Jenli had a decent education because the policy of equal opportunity for girls in China was well established. By the time she went to university in the late seventies, new leaders had opened China to the Western world and to renewal.

I am jolted from daydreaming about Jenli's life when she says, "Next week some Canadian business acquaintances of my husband's are coming to our condo for supper."

"What will you serve them?" I ask, thinking of myself in

her position and knowing that people from all over come to Sichuan for the best food in the world. The prospect scares me, and I tell her so. She tells me she loves to cook and uses no fat, no processed food, and always fresh produce. She makes her own tofu. She is confident and sure of her culinary skills.

Then, out of the blue, she asks, "How often do you clean your house? How long does it take?" She has heard stories too. About Canadian women cleaning a lot. It scares her.

We learn from each other.

Mr. Xu, Jenli, Ross, and I walk down a wide, well-worn gravel path, a testimonial to years of travelling here. The discordant sound of crickets and birds, trees dripping with moisture, and glimpses of ancient temples through nature's magic windows take me back to enchanted places that Du Fu wrote about over a thousand years ago and to fairy tales I read my grandchildren.

My own adventures in writing take me into spaces I didn't know before, and I have new faith in the enduring power of history that is people and their stories.

double happiness

monk at gu si temple

ross with his coach at the cntttc

XVIII

being in another place
(ZHANGDING, CHINA)

*"In a very real sense, the writer writes
in order to teach himself, to understand
himself, to satisfy himself; the
publishing of his ideas, though it brings
gratifications, is a curious anticlimax."*
— ALFRED KAZIN

MAY 2010. The garden pavilions in China remind me of my grandfather's house as I sit here, in the pavilion of the garden at Ross's Ping-Pong camp, properly known as the Chinese National Table Tennis Training Centre, the CNTTTC, in Zhangding. While Ross paddles away for hours each day, I have time to reflect and write.

My grandfather's house at 1 Fallingbrook Road in Toronto is surrounded by grand old oak trees and a white picket fence about five feet high. A half-acre lawn steps down to the bluff, and at the edge is "the teahouse" that overlooks Lake Ontario. The little pavilion, with its breezy Oriental-looking latticework walls and pretty roof, is a magical place for me now in memory, as it was then in play.

Until I was twelve, our family drove every summer from our small company village near Valleyfield, Quebec, to Toronto for our holidays. We would stay one week with my Grandmother Lockhart in a tiny duplex in a working-class district outside the city centre, then the second week at my dad's family's home, Grandfather Phené's house, at the very east end of Queen Street on Lake Ontario.

The two places couldn't have been more different, and we loved them both.

The three of us, my brother Georges, sister Carol, and I, would all be together, without our parents, in Grandma Lockhart's tiny sitting room, where she would spend hours reading to us. She especially loved the writing of Jules Verne and made his science fiction stories like *Around the World in Eighty Days* and *Twenty Thousand Leagues Under the Sea* come alive.

Grandma, though, had her own tales to tell. She loved to write long poems for us, the kind that rhyme, and we would beg her over and over to tell us her stories about growing up "in the olden days." How she was born in Glasgow, Scotland, during Queen Victoria's reign. How her father, a shipbuilder, died of tuberculosis when she was very small.

How her beloved brother Sandy then went to work. How he supported her twelve siblings and her severe mother, who wore the black of mourning all the rest of her life. How she loved school and reading but left school at a young age to work filling tea bags in a factory. How she joined the Salvation Army to see the world and went with them to Canada. How she took a train after she got off the ship and travelled from Halifax to Vancouver before she ditched the Salvation Army and went back to the big city, Toronto.

She told all her stories in a way that made us smile.

She didn't tell us about my Grandfather Lockhart, who was an expert tool and die maker and also a drunk. She didn't talk much about Nancy, her eldest daughter, who loved to sing but died of leukaemia when I was a baby.

When my mother wasn't around, Grandma would serve us tea and brown bread sprinkled with brown sugar that Mother forbade her to give us. Both the tea and the sugar. My tiny, hunchbacked grandmother, with her brisk hobble and trouble-free, sweet laugh, would make fun of Mom and her rules for health and cleanliness. Grandma was our pal, but it was her passion for imagining other times and places that I loved most.

Grandfather's house on the opposite side of town was massive, a mansion, I would say, complete with staff to cook and take care of the property. The house was not old, and he hadn't lived in a mansion all his life. He left France, alone, when he was fourteen to seek his fortune in America. He was the eldest of fourteen starving children, and to his surprise, his starving continued when he first arrived in Atlantic City, New Jersey, via New York City's Ellis Island, and tried to earn a living selling trinkets on the boardwalk. When that didn't work, he went back to New York City and knocked on the door of the first French company he could find. Fortunately, the boss was a compassionate person and gave him a small job in his business, which imported materials for making hats. When Grandfather died in 1953, he was owner of the Toronto franchise Olivier of Canada.

In Toronto, Grandfather was a much-loved leader in the French community, and he was awarded the French Legion of Honour for his work with French immigrants. His home was open to all, and every summer while we were there he would hold parties where some of the ladies wore silk and fancy hats and usually smoked through long, elegant cigarette holders.

"*Dites 'Bonjour, Grandpère,'*" they would say, trying to coax us away from our awful accents and teach us proper French diction, and dignity. Not wishing to be taught French at a party or to be dignified, my brother and sister and I would escape the grown-ups and disappear into the teahouse to create our own magical place to be.

From the table tennis training centre pavilion I can see the roof of another pavilion on a small hill behind a long oxblood-red mud-and-brick wall across the street.

When I went on a two-kilometre exploratory walk to the

opposite end of the wall a couple days ago, I finally reached the entrance to Da Fo Si, Great Buddha Temple, also known as Longxing Temple. I paid for my ticket to get inside the walls and walked another kilometre past five temples and several altars, some dating from AD 500. After some time, I reached the pavilion I had seen from below in the CNTTTC garden. Looking down through the cypress and pine trees, I could see the little pavilion I am in now, where I like to hang out every morning, look at the view, take in the street action, and sometimes write.

The origin of Chinese pavilions, with their graceful upturned tile roofs and latticework, date back to the Zhou dynasty, 1046 to 256 BC. They weren't religious structures but favourite places to sit, rest, and be inspired by the view. Chinese stories tell about scholars and hermits, like Confucius and Du Fu, who sat in places like this to write their poetry and think. Chinese paintings, ancient and new, often show them tucked away in beautiful mountains or beside lakes.

Pavilions, in paintings and in real life, are part of the landscape in China, and when I sit in them, I become part of the scenery. Small children run up to me, stop, stare, giggle, and run away. Bigger children come and say a cool "Hello. How are you?" Older college students often ask politely if I could speak English with them, and the first thing they ask is usually "How old are you?" Women who are about my age sit beside me, without asking anything, to have their picture taken with me. I'm happy to oblige but ask them to take another photo, with my camera.

My pavilion at the CNTTTC is usually private and is surrounded by cherry trees and four large ponds with a 200-metre linear strip of water fountains — ninety-six large spouts and twenty-six smaller ones — which lay dormant until this afternoon.

Then they burst into action.

Into the air, the large fountains shot water twenty metres; the smaller ones bubbled and gurgled. The cherry trees, in full bloom, lit up and started blinking. They were beautiful. It doesn't matter that I hadn't noticed before that they are plastic. Both the trunk and the blossoms.

Shortly afterward, two police vans filled with sleepy-looking cops came and parked at the CNTTTC gate. Then buses and limos arrived. Hundreds of people got out and milled about, some admiring my pavilion. Soldiers in elegant olive and red dress uniform, with white helmets took up positions at the centre's front door.

I knew the people were special. The fountains and cherry trees were the first to give away the secret.

It's not easy for me to understand what's going on in China. It takes all my energy to figure out the Chinese words for "Police" on the vans and even now, after so many years, I can say only a few words in Mandarin and can't read one word easily. Still, I like to know what's going on. Is this occasion to say farewell to the Chinese athletes who are leaving for next week's Table Tennis World Cup in Moscow? I've observed that elite athletes are treated with tremendous respect and reverence, almost like that accorded to Buddha. The Chinese National Table Tennis Team have been training to be champions their whole lives, and their presence here at the CNTTTC with us is shrouded in secrecy and intrigue. As foreigners, we're not allowed to enter the posh, state-of-the-art building on campus where they are training.

Could Ross and I be spies?

"Do you play?" a man says smoothly in perfect English, shortly after Ross joins me in the pavilion.

I jump with a start. I hadn't seen him as Ross and I stood watching, trying to figure out what's happening with all the fuss. The man is too close. And disarming. We've hardly heard English for a month.

Who is this guy? Why is he in this place? My place, my pavilion. His smile is honest and his appearance is that of a person carefully put together. His neatly pressed black trousers and crisp white shirt are a strange contrast to our sports gear.

Taken aback, Ross says, "I'm sorry. What did you say? I don't understand."

"Do you play?" he repeats smoothly, curiously.

Play what? I think.

"Well, yes, I'm a beginner. I'm here to practise," Ross says.

"Are you National Team?" the man asks with disbelief.

"No, no. I have a Chinese coach. I'm here to practise," Ross explains.

"But I don't understand. Why are you at this place?"

"But why are you here, in this place?" I interrupt them, trying not to be too cheeky. I need to stop the way this conversation is going, I tell myself. Even I don't really understand why I am at this place. Could I have known when I was imagining other places in my grandfather's tea pavilion that in 2010 I would be spending two weeks at Ping-Pong camp in China?

"For competition," the man says carefully. "I am at this place for competition, with the Ministry of Trade and Commerce. With the government."

"You mean the Chinese government. Like the one in Beijing?" I ask. Like on Tiananmen Square, I think to myself, and then tell myself to hurry up and figure out what this guy wants with us, before his next question.

He gives Ross his business card — "Mr. Li. Researcher, Department of Treaty and Law, Ministry of Trade and Commerce." I make a mental note: *Yet another Mr. Li in China; there are millions and millions of Mr. Lis.* Mr. Li explains that he spent some time on business in Ottawa in May last year when the tulips were blooming. He says he loved Canada.

"Now," he says, "I am here to play Ping-Pong."

He explains that representatives from various government ministries are at the CNTTTC this weekend for a match. Competing with each other helps them learn to work together.

Not bad, I think and then croon, "Oh, you mean like team-building. Like golf at home. Oh. What a good idea."

I breathe a sigh of liberation.

When Ross first proposed coming here to play Ping-Pong, I balked at his idea. Then when a young friend, the son of Ross's client in China, called to invite us to his wedding in

Chengdu, I made up my mind to come too. A few days in Sichuan at the wedding, a week in Beijing to visit parts we hadn't fully explored on previous visits — Marco Polo Bridge and some lesser-visited parts of the Forbidden City — and three weeks to hang out and write while Ross practised his table tennis would be a perfect retreat from the monotony of Calgary's elusive spring. And a chance for me to retreat to my childhood pleasures while I write.

Now each morning I sit in the little pavilion in the CNTTTC's garden while Ross practises his paddling with his young but expert Chinese table tennis coach. I think a lot about how I came to be in this place and like it. I didn't come for Ping-Pong. That was Ross's reason. I was enticed by the adventure of being in another place, and, as the famous literary critic Alfred Kazin said, to write in order to understand myself, teach myself, and satisfy myself. Kazin also said that although publishing is gratifying, it is an anticlimax. I'm not ready for the anticlimax.

I wonder how Marco Polo felt when he finished his book.

dungarpur

XIX

yoga, a giant pangolin, and jazz
(INDIA)

*F*OR AS LONG as I can remember, I've travelled India, although vicariously, through books. Marco Polo might be my muse. When my own story about the Silk Road began almost half a century ago now, Ross and I had to abort our plan to work and travel in India because of a war. When we finally got there for the first time, in 1994, I was involved with UNICEF and went on a tour to learn about children's health and education.

This time, I'm in India to rest and to try to fuse the information I've gathered over the years so I can find a way to close my story.

By the time Marco began his return voyage to Venice, more than two decades after he set out, he was a different person. He'd had twenty-four years' experience visiting places in the Far East, and when he sailed around the coast of India aboard a merchant ship on his way home, he was more open to diversity and was able to relax and admire what he saw. His stories draw his readers' attention to India's geography and natural phenomena. "Everything is so different," he says over and over. He describes peculiar animals, birds, flora, food, and drink. He's fascinated by the variety of people, their languages and customs, local arts and crafts. He tells the reader of an India so vast and complicated it would take him another year to recount all the stories.

I'm in awe of Marco. Like him, I've changed over the years. Now I'm here to savour whatever I can find in India. A yoga practise might be a good starting point; after all, yoga originated in India long before Marco came. Millions of people who live here now practise it. I'm willing to give it a try; it fits with my travel focus of fusing information, in this case the body, the mind, and the spirit. With time flashing by comes a will to try anything to stay in life-can-last-forever mode.

My private yoga practise will be in the old former hunting lodge on the property of the palace-like hotel in which we are staying, a fact that is somewhat off-putting for me. It is very different from the pristine yoga studio I go to at home, with forty other participants. My thoughts are mixed; I begin to wonder why I want to do this. But here I am. In Rajasthan. In my expedition-weight long underwear (damn, why did I leave my yoga gear in Calgary?), waiting for the yoga lesson and my introduction to India.

Kumar, impeccably dressed in pressed white cotton yoga pyjamas, is expressionless. "Come," he says, leading the way across a park alongside an environmental reserve next to the hunting lodge. And the yoga mats. I stumble along behind him, uttering a few Canadian pleasantries to try to take the edge off and, perhaps, pry a smile out of his poker face. But he is steadfast. This tall man with a perfect, straight spine, neatly cropped black hair, and tidy mustache is dedicated and wants me to take his instruction seriously.

Somehow my long underwear gives me a comfy-homey feeling that overpowers the discomfort I feel when I'm totally out of place. The peacocks and peahens on the path scuttle away, screaming their sympathy, "Help. Help." Are they crying out that they're here to help me feel safe?

At the entrance to the lodge, Mr. Singh, the eighty-year-old turbaned caretaker I met yesterday, claps his hands to his heart in prayer before smiling through his magnificent white handlebar mustache. "*Namaste*," he says, welcoming me before he leads me up a zigzagging narrow staircase, designed 200 years ago to confuse intruders on their way up to the second floor and mixing me up even more.

In the maharajahs' days of glory this lodge would have been surrounded by a hundred trumpeting elephants waiting to take hunters out to the adjacent forest to shoot tigers, Mr. Singh remembers. I like Mr. Singh's presence. He told me he belongs to the Rajputs, a historically fierce warrior caste; now he's here to protect me.

At the top of the stairs is a small stone terrace overlooking the environmental reserve. My yoga mat has been neatly placed on the shiny, cool floor facing the forest.

I take a deep breath. Fresh, warm breezes, punctuated with the scent of bougainvillea and hibiscus, soothe me.

A deep blue sky frames tight green clusters of the Aravalli Mountain Range surrounding Lake Pichola and Udaipur's famous white marble palace. It is late in the afternoon, and the day cools as the hot sun begins to sink into the hills.

"Take your place. Your mat is your own private space."

"Thank you." I take my place. I stand on the mat. So far so good.

Kumar kneels and nods, affirming that I should do the same.

I kneel. My crackly knees break the quiet. I stifle a nervous, self-conscious giggle.

"Relaxxxxxx. Close your eyes, Mrs. Hayes. *Ommmmm.* Say *ommmmm* with me," he says almost too quietly for me to hear but with a definite no-nonsense tone. I do my best. I try to keep my eyes shut, but I have an urgent need to know what's happening. Where am I? What's going on? What do I do now?

"Enjooooyyy the practise," Kumar chants. I make an effort to calm myself.

I'm told the position of stillness is yoga's most difficult. And for me it is impossible.

I open my eyes.

The air, the sweet smell of the park, and the sun beginning to settle down behind the hills are background for a strange slow movement of some sort at the edge of the park, behind Kumar. Kumar's eyes are still closed, but mine are wide open now.

Something deep within me says, "Be still, Nancy. Do not speak. This moment is special for you." A peculiar beast about the size of a large Canadian pig emerges from the bushes and shuffles along the edge of the environmental reserve. From the tip of its long narrow head to the bottom of its elongated fat tail, the creature is covered with huge, shiny, smooth scales the pale colour of Rajasthan's dry earth. Slowly, surely, it then waddles away and disappears into the forest.

I am calmed, in awe. What have I seen?

I return to my muse, Marco, the model traveller of 700 years ago. "Remember this gift and take it with you," the voice inside me says. Would I have missed the pangolin had I not been in pursuit of stillness, relaxing and enjoying a quiet yoga practise while I'm here?

A few days later, a biologist at Kanhe National Park, one of the largest tiger reserves in India, tells me that the giant Indian pangolin is a rare sight, perhaps more exceptional than seeing a tiger in the wild. Genetically distinct, the animal, also known as a giant scaly anteater, is endangered, like the Bengal tiger, because of hunting and destruction of its habitat. Illegal trafficking of the pangolin has been an additional problem for a long time. In 1820 King George III of Britain was presented with an unusual coat of armour made of its scales. In China the meat is considered a great delicacy, and the scales of the pangolin are used for medicinal properties.

A day later we are seeing the land by van. The traffic is hair-raising. "Have you heard yet the three things you must have to drive safely in India?" our driver chuckles. "Good brakes. Good horn . . ."

"And the third?" I ask.

"Good luck."

I quickly decide to save myself from the terror of driving in India by looking only out the van's side windows and only when necessary. The van brakes and swerves around elephants and camels with wide loads of wood and rebar strapped on their backs. We honk at India's holy cows lying not quite on the median of the new four-lane highway, but in the shade of beautiful bougainvillea landscaping. Through the Aravalli Mountains we twist and blast our way around blind corners. I note that Hindu temples are strategically situated, and they prompt me to squeeze my eyes shut and ask the powers that be for a long life.

In due course, we swing south off the highway and career along a gravel road surrounded by forest reserve owned by the Maharajah of Dungarpur. Twenty minutes later, we veer off through a gap in the trees and come to a quiet stop in front of the royal residence, our hotel for a few days. Our driver phoned a few minutes ago, and the maharajah's nephew is waiting for us. After a few quick *namastes* and welcomes, his assistant, the hotel manager, leads us toward our room.

"This is the office," he says, as we pass beneath the stuffed heads of four tigers, six wild boars, several deer, and one sloth bear. "We have wireless in this room and at the pool," he adds.

We walk into the adjacent palace courtyard and around

an exquisitely carved temple surrounded by water to one more interior courtyard. In the middle is an enormous white marble dining table set for thirty people. Carved into the centre of the table is a long rectangular pool filled with lotus flowers and goldfish. "This is where you will eat breakfast and dinner," the manager tells us.

There are surprises everywhere, giving me that being-in-a-surreal-world feeling again.

The maharajah shot ninety-nine tigers in his day, and they are all here, almost hidden, their heads staked high on the walls. The family now pride themselves on being conservationists. A team of young museum curators is in the ballroom with ancient royal clothing organized on the floor, ready to catalog for a family museum. At the door there is a fleet of mountain bikes ready for guests to ride around the estate's vast nature reserve. The tigers are gone, but I've been told there are a few deer, fox, and wild boar bounding about.

A curtained archway behind an immense locked wooden door leads into a gigantic room. Ours. Filled with an eclectic assortment of memorabilia from the sixties, it has the stamp of our home in Calgary. A low arch leads to a marble balcony overlooking Lake Galbsagar and its finely crafted temple island in the centre.

This is my place. My armchair is waiting.

Lake Galbsagar is a mirror; the sound of swarming water birds — herons, storks, cranes, egrets, ducks — fills the still, late-afternoon air. My maharajah, Ross, scouts out his battered blue metal water bottle and pours for us. India's favourite. Black Dog scotch whiskey.

Am I in heaven?

"Yoo-hoo. Hello, there. Be sure to come for before-dinner cocktails with us at seven o'clock," the maharajah's niece-in-law calls up to us from the lakeside path below and waves. The royal family's friendliness is infectious, and we are eager to join them. Sober or not.

Later, with difficulty, we work our way through the dark, back under the stuffed heads, the dim eco lamps, and down the stairs to the big dining room. Candles fill the courtyard, but no one is here.

"Hello. Where is everybody?"

A young man with a tall white chef's hat peers around a partition at the back. "No. No. It's not here. Follow." He leads us through a giant doorway into a damp muddy field. The night is black even though the stars are out and the moon is full behind the trees. Something alive scuttles across the mud in front of me. I stifle a scream. It's a chicken. In spite of my fancy new, but cruelly uncomfortable, sandals, I tumble through what appears to be a vegetable garden. I struggle to keep my culturally appropriate Rajasthan *bandhani*, a colourful tie-dye sarong, wrapped around me as I trudge through the "we water at night" save-the-environment mud.

In the distance, I see a dim light shining from another one of those low-watt eco bulbs hanging on the end wall of a long shed, which Ross says is the old stable. I'm still struggling to keep my clothes wrapped while choking back laughter at the ridiculous situation I find myself in. Why didn't I wear jeans?

"Hey. Stop a minute," Ross croaks in a hushed tone. "What's that I hear?"

The noise—it sounds like snare drums—intensifies as we get closer to the shed.

The door opens. Louis Armstrong's gravelly voice resonates through the old stable: "What a Wonderful World." The maharajah's family is beaming with delight. I recognize the manager, even though he's wearing a tux now.

Where are we? I'm confused. Then I realize this is a surprise the maharajah has for us. It is his new museum, and it is filled with elegantly spotlit, gleaming, like-new antique cars.

The family walks with us between the rows of vintage cars to the end of the old stable, where we enter a glass-walled room.

We sit down at a sixties-style bar. The crack of snare drums, the tingle of cymbals vibrating, the soft rhythmic strike of piano, and the silk-smooth saxophone playing the melody in "Take Five" bring a flood of memories.

Start a little conversation now.
Just take five.
Stop your busy day and come out to see that I'm alive.
Just take five.

It is the music we listened to often in 1965, as we dreamed of travelling the Silk Road, composed by saxophonist Paul Desmond while he was touring with the Dave Brubeck

Quartet along segments of the Silk Road in Turkey, India, Pakistan, and Afghanistan. "Take Five" was inspired by the melody nomads played one day as they walked by the open door flap of Desmond's tent. Later, when the group finished their tour, Dave Brubeck and his wife wrote lyrics.

> *So why is it that you keep going there? people still ask me.*
> *Because I can't close my story. Yet.*
> *I say.*
> *Just stop your busy day and take five.*
> *It's a wonderful world.*

udaipur

walking to the yoga pavilion

238

ABOUT THE AUTHOR

*N*ANCY M. HAYES is a nurse by profession and a writer by avocation. She grew up in Quebec, graduated from the
Montreal General Hospital School of Nursing, and completed a diploma in public health nursing at McGill University.
Later she received a bachelor's degree in community health
(Concordia University) and a master's degree in nursing,
maternal child health (University of Calgary).

Nancy and her husband, Ross (see next page), have
three children and four grandchildren, and live in Calgary,
Alberta. They have also lived in England, Jamaica, the
United States, and, briefly, in Afghanistan (see Chapter XII).
It is a privilege for Nancy to be able to support education for
girls and women in Afghanistan by donating the proceeds
from *Weaving Threads* to Canadian Women for Women in
Afghanistan. Volunteering has always been an important
part of her life: Her first position was as president of her
high school Junior Red Cross, and many years later she
served as volunteer president of UNICEF Canada. Nancy
loves spending time in the mountains, where she hikes,
skis, bicycles, and writes.

ROSS E. HAYES (illustrator) grew up in Montreal and graduated with a bachelor's degree in architecture from Mc-Gill University. He then went to Harvard University, where he completed a master's degree in architecture (urban design) because he wanted to design overall communities as well as individual buildings. As a director of IBI Group, a large multidisciplinary design firm, he was able to bring both interests to bear on projects in Canada, the United States, China, Europe, and Israel. He is volunteer president of Alberta TrailNet, working on the development of a trail system to link communities across Canada. Ross enjoys hiking and skiing in the Rockies, table tennis, and cycling. His lifelong interest in photography and sketching adds to his enjoyment of travel.

CPSIA information can be obtained at www.ICGtesting.com
Printed in the USA
LVOW100714100513

333100LV00002B/10/P